P9-DDF-431

Keeping COOL on the HOT Seat

Dealing Effectively with the Media in Times of Crisis

Judith C. Hoffman

FOUR C'S PUBLISHING COMPANY
Highland Mills, New York

Copyright © 2001 Judith Hoffman
First Printing 2001
Second Printing 2001
Third Printing 2004, Revised, Third Edition
Fourth Printing 2006

All rights reserved. No part of this book may be reproduced or transmitted in any form or by any means, electronic or mechanical, including photocopying, recording, or by any information storage and retrieval system, without permission in writing from the publisher.

Published and distributed by:
    4 C's Publishing Company
    25 Jones Drive
    Highland Mills, NY 10930
    Phone: 845-928-8239
    Fax: 845-928-3463
    e-mail: jchent@fcc.net

Hoffman, Judith C.
    Keeping cool on the hot seat : dealing effectively with the media in times of crisis / Judith C. Hoffman. —Highland Mills, NY : Four C's Pub. Co., 2001

        p. cm.

    ISBN 0-9709014-0-2 (pbk.)
        1. Corporations—Public relations. 2. Mass media and business.
        3. Public relations. 4. Industrial publicity. I.
        Title. II. Dealing effectively with the media in times of crisis

HD59 .H64 2001   2001-87778
659 .2/85—dc21   CIP

08 07 06 05 04 • 5 4
Project Coordination by Jenkins Group, Inc. • www.bookpublishing.com

Printed in the United States of America

Dedication

To my Dad, Carl F. Cooke
who taught me to believe in
God and my dreams.
I am just sorry that he did not
live long enough
to see this dream come true.

Contents

Acknowledgments

There is a saying "That which does not kill us makes us stronger." I certainly believe it is true that we learn the most from our most difficult experiences. From that perspective, then, I should acknowledge here those who provided me with opportunities to learn all that I know about dealing with crises. Many of these people remain nameless to me, but they include: the railroad crew whose actions resulted in tipping over a railcar full of a hazardous chemical on our company property; the fellow who called in the bomb scare; the sub-contractor who caused an ammonia leak in the boiler room causing a plant evacuation; and workers who, in the 1950's, disposed of materials in ways that are now known to be environmentally unacceptable. From each of these situations I learned important lessons that have formed the foundation of my consulting business. Now I can share with the managers of other companies what I learned the hard way.

One to whom I owe a special debt of gratitude is James L. Lukaszewski, founder and Chairman of the Lukaszewski Group. Jim was the first crisis management consultant I ever met. We talked to him when the company I worked for faced an especially difficult situation. I learned a great deal from reading his materials and discussing situations with him, particularly when I started my own consulting business. Much of the material in this book is based on principles he taught.

I also want to acknowledge my clients, past and present. Each time I did a workshop, I learned more about how the principles of dealing with the media during a crisis played out in their industry. It is so wonderful that I now count many of these current and former clients among my friends. My thanks to the following people who took the time to review portions of the manuscript and gave me their valuable insights and encouragement: Glenda Akins, John D. Beckett, John Nichols, William Gossett, Ed Kelley, Tedd Ahlberg, Jay Richard, Bill Mackay, John Checklick, Bob Hannan, Iris Sandow, Mike Smith, and Lou Heimbach. Another colleague who was especially generous with her time was Carolyn Harshman. Her insights regarding municipalities and emergency responders were particularly helpful.

An author is fortunate to find a great editor. I was truly blessed. While spokesperson for the chemical manufacturing company, I came into frequent contact with Bob Riemann, a business reporter for the local daily newspaper. Over sixteen years, we developed a relationship of mutual trust and respect. Three years after I started my own consulting business, Bob did the same. Knowing his ability to tighten copy, I asked for his help. His perspective as an experienced journalist was an added benefit. This was later augmented when Karen Friedman, a former TV reporter, also agreed to look over portions of the manuscript.

Then I was further blessed to have a daughter, Cheri, who is continuing to develop her God-given talents as a freelance writer. She was willing to proofread and offer editorial suggestions that improved the manuscript significantly.

Finally, I want to express my appreciation to my husband, Cris. When he retired last fall after teaching junior high for 30 years, we had visions of travelling and relaxing. We found that life activities became divided into "B.B." and "A.B." (Before the Book and After the Book). My thanks for his hard work editing and proofreading as well as his patience and, as always, his love and support.

Foreword

I know what it is like to be on the "hot seat" when a crisis has occurred. I can recall the anxiety I felt when I heard that the TV reporters were going to be in the lobby in fifteen minutes with their camera crew, ready for my statement.

If you dread being the spokesperson in such an incident—or even if you are only somewhat uncomfortable—this book has been written for you. Over my 16 years as the media spokesperson for a chemical manufacturing company, I learned a great deal about how to work with the media during difficult times. An overturned rail-car, a bomb threat, the painstakingly slow clean-up of an inactive hazardous waste site, and the odorous emissions that caused the evacuation of local schools are vivid in my memory. Talk about your hands-on training!

During my career, I did a lot of things wrong. When I first took on the role as spokesperson, I had never had any media training. I said some things I wish I had not. I forgot to say things I wanted to say. But from those mistakes I learned lessons I have never forgotten. To increase my knowledge, I attended seminars and listened to other peoples' experiences—good and bad. I read books and journal articles and immersed myself in crisis case studies.

One day, the president of the company asked me to put together a workshop on how to communicate in a crisis. Officers from corporate headquarters attended. They liked it so much that they asked me to present the seminar for their other subsidiaries. Feedback was positive. My colleagues were complimentary, saying they found the course to be full of practical tips and techniques they could put into action immediately. I found that I loved teaching these workshops. In 1995 I started my own consulting business centered on media and community relations consulting.

It quickly became apparent that this type of crisis communications training was needed in ALL kinds of organizations. Remember some of the stories behind these headlines?

- Hazardous materials spill causes evacuation of 2-mile area
- Hospital amputates wrong leg
- Teacher/priest/rabbi/minister accused of sexual misconduct
- Death caused by emergency responders' delay or mistake
- Salmonella poisoning causes recall of two million chickens
- Company accused of putting profits before consumer safety
- Fire in college dormitory kills three students
- Health care facility loses accreditation
- Worker goes berserk and kills three
- Civil rights group calls for boycott of company products
- Major employer announces massive lay-off
- Local company plane crashes killing five senior officers
- Electrical generating plant accused of price gouging
- Fuel oil delivery made to home without a tank
- Family of nursing home patient sues for negligence
- Favorite Christmas toy subject of recall
- Bank accused of discriminating in granting loans
- Sexual harassment lawsuit lodged
- Infant dies in child care center
- Power outages leave thousands in the dark for days
- Executive of not-for-profit is paid excessive salary

Many of my clients asked if I had any of this material written down. I provided seminar workbooks and handed out some articles I had written, but they wanted more. This was the genesis of this book.

Many of my competitors in the media training business are former journalists. I, on the other hand, come to this business from the other end of the microphone. Like those of you for whom this book is written, businesses leaders, emergency officials and not-for-profit managers, I was "in the trenches." This is not theoretical stuff. This is reality in a world where crises make dramatic headlines every day.

I originally wrote this book in the spring of 2001. Who would have ever thought then that we were on the threshold of some of the most dramatic crises of all time: the attacks of 9/11, the imploding of Enron and other business giants, the scandals in the Catholic Church, and the legal troubles of famous people like Martha Stewart? These things begged for comment; hence this 2004 revision.

My hope is that you will put this book in a place where it will be easy to find when (not IF) something unexpected or unfortunate happens to your organization. I hope that you will have contracted with a media training professional who can work with you and your management team BEFORE the media shows up at your door. If this is not the case, chances are good you will say and do the wrong things (or neglect to say and do the right things). The result will be to cause the crisis to be worse and last longer, costing you countless hours of pain, aggravation, and non-productivity, not to mention money, that could have been spent more beneficially.

If you have had professional media training, and can put into action the advice in this book, you should have the confidence to allow you to step in front of the reporters, massed microphones, or TV cameras and represent your organization positively.

Good luck!

Disclaimer

The content of this book is based on years of personal experience and has been validated by public affairs and media representatives as well as managers of many different organizations. However, there can be no guarantee that the advice contained here will be exactly right for every situation. Counsel should be sought from trusted crisis management or public relations professionals and legal advisors who are familiar with your organization and your specific set of circumstances.

Preparing for a Crisis

The companies that have not paid enough—or any—attention to thinking through what they would do if a crisis were to erupt tomorrow are doomed to pay dearly for this oversight. They will pay in terms of pain, aggravation, stress, innumerable lost man-hours, and a black mark against their corporate reputation. In addition, they run the risk of serious negative impacts to their bottom line ($$$).

On the other hand, those organizations which have spent time preparing for a crisis will either be able to prevent it entirely or will be ready to say and do the right things to shorten its life cycle. They will get back to work faster with their corporate reputation intact or even enhanced.

The engineers who designed the Titanic were so sure of everything, they didn't think it necessary to provide enough lifeboats for all the passengers.

When Something Goes Wrong

Perhaps you've heard the story about the newest airplane built with the latest technology. On its maiden flight, the automated message played for the passengers ended with, "And so, nothing can go wrong... can go wrong... can go wrong."

Every day when you show up at work something can go wrong. Only those managers who insist on being foolishly optimistic think they manage perfectly, that equipment is infallible, and that their employees will never make a mistake in judgment. Even if you don't actually *do* anything wrong, all it takes is one allegation or one lawsuit to seriously damage your corporate reputation and waste inordinate amounts of time and resources.

If anything *does* go wrong, don't be surprised to find the media at your door. Today, the proliferation of media channels has created a hunger for news. Controversy, drama, and confrontation make news. If you have been in denial, acting as though nothing bad would ever happen, you will be at a definite disadvantage when trying to respond quickly and effectively to media inquiries.

Thinking Proactively

Make no mistake. Responding **quickly** is important. It has often been said that organizations have 1-2 hours to demonstrate that they will gain control of the crisis. If you have done no preparation for a crisis, never considered the various types of things that could go wrong in your business and what you would do about it, you will waste those first 1-2 hours. As a result, you will find yourself being reactive and chasing the crisis. You will miss your chance to make that all-important positive first impression.

Smart organizations take a proactive approach. They take time to seriously think through, as a management team, the types of things that could develop into a crisis. It is not hard. Just get the key players together and spend a half-hour brainstorming about "What could go wrong around here?"

Don't limit yourself to the obvious. Almost all the groups I have worked with in teaching the workshop "Coaching to Meet the Press and Other Hostile Audiences" can easily come up with a half dozen possible crises. "Fire, explosion, spill" are almost always the first things mentioned by my friends in the chemical industry and other manufacturers.

With nudging, they can expand on that list to include: industrial accidents which cause injury or death, lack of pre-planning or coordination, bomb threats, regulatory agency inspections and fines, product contamination or liability, labor disputes, neighbors unhappy about noise, dust, traffic, odor, emissions, etc.

There are even more potential crises. What if the officers of your organization embezzled funds? What if a natural disaster hit? Or if you had an assault in your school? How would you handle a community protest at your gate? What could you say if an employee were caught dealing drugs to young children? How would you react if an employee went berserk and killed another? (Seems far fetched, but homicide is the third leading cause of death in the

American workplace today!)

The media would jump on any of these stories. If you have not thought through what your first actions would be and how you would phrase your initial response, you could easily have a full-blown crisis on your hands. It could negatively affect employee morale, your corporate reputation, and even your bottom line.

Taking Preventative Steps

Once you have identified all of the possible crises, you must take the next step. You must believe that the scenarios you listed are possible and then discuss as a group what could be done to *prevent* the problem. Look at various aspects of your operation. Can you beef up security, develop a plan of action for product contamination/liability issues, review your human resources policies, institute adequate accounting safeguards, update your emergency plan, increase labor/management harmony, or enhance your community relations outreach efforts?

One person should be designated to lead a task force on each area in which you have determined you are vulnerable. He or she should be tasked to come up with a plan for avoiding the crisis. Implement it. Develop and agree upon the initial response plan for each item. (See Chapter 4 for more details.)

If, despite your best efforts to prevent it, a crisis *does* occur in one of these areas, the fact that you have discussed the issue as a management group will give you a head start in implementing your response strategy. You will be better able to take quick and appropriate action. As a result, you will be viewed as an organization that is both responsible to the public and responsive to the media.

Do not allow your organization to wallow in denial, repeating day after lucky day, "Nothing can go wrong here." Chances are very good that, some day, something *will* go wrong. If you have spent time discussing the possibilities and planning how to handle them, you have the best chance of surviving the crisis with your organization's good reputation intact and your bottom line unaffected.

Checking Your Organization's Moral Compass

All of the above assumes that your organization is trying to do the right thing. But we now know, only too well, that this is not always the case.

This book was initially published in the spring of 2001. Looking back, that was a time of relative innocence, when the leaders of business and industry were generally respected and some of our government agencies were more highly regarded. Front page stories in 2002 tore away the veil and proved some of our business leaders of multi-million dollar empires were more interested in lining their own pockets than with the well-being of their employees and shareholders. Post 9/11 investigations highlighted the fact that the CIA and the FBI were more interested in preserving their individual powers than working together for the common good. Added to all this was the continuing saga of the betrayal of trust of some of the country's most high-ranking religious leaders who were more interested in preserving their reputation and their coffers than in protecting innocent children.

Powerful lessons can be learned by looking at these situations (see Section VIII). Here I just want to say that no book on dealing with the media can tell you how to make these types of situations turn out to be anything less than what they are—an unmitigated disaster. Before you step to the microphone to defend your organization, make sure they are trying to DO the right thing!

2

What Is a Crisis?

A ll of you face problems. Operational incidents. People problems. Sales and marketing issues. Financial difficulties. Differences of opinion or misunderstandings with customers, shareholders, employees, or Board members. Solving these problems is part of a manager's job.

A crisis is quite different. It is a problem of such magnitude that it interrupts your ability to do business. It is a critical turning point. It affects the way you are perceived by the public and other important audiences. Just think about the Firestone tire crisis and how that negatively affected not only them but also the Ford Motor Company.

Crisis as "Danger"

Interestingly enough, there are two separate Chinese characters that make up the English word "crisis." (See Figure 1.) The first is "danger." It is quite obvious that a crisis poses danger. It could be an actual threat to human safety or health. In less extreme cases, it could still mean grave problems for your organization's reputation.

Crisis as "Opportunity"

The second of the two Chinese characters, however, is "opportunity."

At first glance, combining opposite concepts like danger and opportunity seems to be quite a stretch. Nonetheless, it is true. There are organizations which have not only survived the dangers posed by a crisis, but have actually enhanced their corporate reputations because of the responsible, responsive and competent way they handled it.

Figure 1

The classic example taught in many public relations courses is the case study of the Tylenol capsules laced with cyanide that caused the death of seven people in the Chicago area. After an initial loss of profits when Johnson & Johnson removed the Tylenol products from store shelves, the company rebounded strongly. Within a short time, they recaptured their previous market share. The public gave the company credit for living up to the written corporate Values Statement which said the health and well-being of their customers was their first priority. When the crisis occurred, Johnson & Johnson backed up these words quickly with action. Consequently, Tylenol's brand name was secure. Today people think of Johnson & Johnson as a responsible corporate citizen. This was a clear case of turning danger into opportunity.

What About Your Organization?

Most days you operate with a low profile. Some companies are almost invisible to the general public. Or, if the public knows they exist, community residents don't pay much attention to them. Members of the public have their own set of problems. As long as you don't directly impact their lives, they are content to co-exist with you in their community. But if something drastic happens—an accident at your facility that threatens people or the environment or a publicized allegation of wrongdoing—the spotlight is suddenly shining on you.

The way you react to the crisis is played out in the media for everyone to see. How you respond in those first moments and hours will be noticed and remembered. It could affect the way people perceive your organization—either positively or negatively—perhaps for years to come. For this reason, you must make sure you and your senior management team go through an effective crisis management training program.

The Importance of a Positive Mind Set

When a crisis erupts, it may not come naturally for you to look at it from the perspective of "Wow, look at this OPPORTUNITY we have!" However, if you can remember these Chinese characters and understand what they mean, it can help you face the crisis with a more positive attitude. It can provide you with a mind set that will help you do what you should in the best long-term interests of your organization **and** your community.

"The irony of the 'Information Age' is that it has given new respectability to uninformed opinion."

—*Veteran reporter John Lawton speaking at a meeting of the American Association of Broadcast Journalists (1995)*

3

Categories of Crisis

Basically, you can break crises down into five different categories.

Sudden Emergencies

When your phone rings at 2 a.m., you know it can't be good news. Your first thoughts go to your family members. When you pick it up and hear someone from work on the other end, what type of message do you expect to hear? A fire? An industrial accident that has injured an employee? A rape on your campus? A transportation accident? What is it that you fear the most? These emergencies are characterized by "speed of onset." One minute everything seems to be fine. The next, your whole world has been turned upside down.

Once the immediate physical danger is past, there will be lots of people who will want to know what happened and why. Repairing relationships and regaining the trust of your community—especially if the incident affected people outside your organization—could take days, weeks, months, or even years of work.

"Creeping crises"

More often than not, when I ask participants in my workshops to brainstorm about what could go wrong in their organization, managers give the most obvious answers, usually related to the sudden emergency type of crisis.

Then I prime the pump by showing them actual headlines of crises. "Oh, yes," they say. "We could have a lawsuit brought by an employee for racial discrimination or sexual harassment. We could be accused of violating a regulation that might bring a fine. We could receive a bomb threat made by someone who was unhappy with our organization. A disgruntled employee could claim we had an unsafe workplace. Our product could get contaminated, causing customer complaints. We could even lose the business of our major customer because we did not efficiently handle these complaints that had been brought to our attention on several occasions."

All of these are examples of what I call "creeping crises." They may have begun small, but they eventually grew to crisis proportions because they were not handled expeditiously.

A female employee complains to her supervisor about off-color jokes. But the supervisor is busy with high priority projects and deadlines. He doesn't have time to get involved with "this stuff." He figures everything will probably blow over. It is nothing to bother the higher-ups about.

A few weeks later, the woman reports a similar incident to the supervisor. Still, nothing is done to investigate the allegations. The woman is told she is just being too sensitive to good-natured fun. When a third complaint goes unanswered, the woman files formal charges against the company, naming the first-line supervisor, the Director of Human Resources, and the Plant Manager. You have to engage a lawyer. The media finds out about it and you suddenly appear on the front page of your local newspaper.

But is it really "sudden?" Not at all. The problem was

minimized, ignored, and avoided. It went from a manageable internal issue to a real crisis that could threaten your external corporate reputation. It could end up costing your company dearly in terms of its bottom line.

If you doubt that we are talking about serious money, just look at Figure 2 for average settlements or judgments in cases like these.

Figure 2

THE HIGH COST OF EMPLOYEE LAWSUITS

Mounting a defense (just through complaint filing stage) can cost $35,000

Litigation defense: takes inordinate amounts of management time and energy and can even financially cripple a business

If you lose, average jury awards run:

Wrongful termination	**$532,000**
Age discrimination	**$450,000**
Sex discrimination	**$255,000**

Predictable Crises

There are crises that you can almost count on. The one that springs most easily to mind relates to labor issues. If a union contract expires on January 31st, and management knows they are going to have to hold the line or ask for givebacks, they can be sure that the union will not take this lying down. While negotiations are going on, management needs to be preparing a strike contingency plan. They should also be brushing up on their media training skills. They can be assured they'll get a call from the press just before and just after the deadline and frequently thereafter until a settlement is reached.

Another time when media attention is focused on you is on the anniversary of a memorable negative event. If your organization had a major incident (especially if someone were killed), the press may well want to do a story. As that date approaches, you would be well served to give some serious thought to how you would respond to a media inquiry. This can certainly be a case where you can turn "danger" into "opportunity." If you have compiled a list of things you have done since the incident to improve your operations or to minimize the chance that such a thing could happen again, you may have an excellent story to tell.

Crises Caused by Dumb Decisions

Many times crises are not caused by external forces. They come from someone who is not seeing the big picture. By considering only the short-term financial impact, they end up giving the organization a black eye that has longer lasting impacts on their bottom line and corporate reputation.

Firestone Wilderness tires come to mind. At some point as this problem began to unfold, someone made the decision that it would be too costly to recall tires and settle a few lawsuits. They decided to take a hard line, try to shift the blame to the Ford Motor Company (great way to solidify relationships with one of your best customers!), and hunker down until it blew over. The result? Over 187 deaths and many more serious injuries traced to tire failures and rollovers. Numerous multi-million dollar lawsuits have been filed. This dumb decision brought about the resignation of the head of the Firestone company, caused consumers to shy away from both Firestone tires and Ford Explorers, and made those companies the subject of numerous unflattering cartoons and scathing editorials that labeled the executives as criminals, among other things.

"CyberCrises"

The Internet has had a dramatic impact on media relations, enough to be the subject of an entire book. In terms of crisis management, it means several things. First, old ideas of deadlines are obsolete when dealing with a communications vehicle that can transmit 24 hours a day and 7 days a week. Almost instantaneous answers are asked for. This means that, more than ever, organizational leaders have to be highly skilled so they can respond appropriately and very quickly.

The Internet Age also has brought with it a new type of crisis. Rogue web sites can spring up quickly, posted by anyone who is upset with your organization. It only takes one person—a disgruntled employee, an unhappy customer, a shell-shocked investor—to start the ball rolling. Word spreads quickly through e-mail and more and more people visit the web site. The company's name is dragged through the mud in chat rooms. Rumors and unsubstantiated allegations are stated as facts and there is NO standard of ethics. No Great Webmaster in the Sky requires those who post things to verify the truthfulness of what they say. Veteran reporter John Lawton, when speaking to the American Association of Broadcast Journalists, said, "The irony of the Information Age is that it has given new respectability to uninformed opinion."

The Association of Flaming Ford Owners used their web site to hammer the Ford Motor Company over what they alleged were dangerous defects. An activist group took on McDonald's. They gave worldwide negative publicity to a lawsuit that McDonald's had filed against two people in England who had distributed a flyer entitled "What's Wrong with McDonald's?" It could have been a one-day story, but when McDonald's decided to sue the two people, the story went worldwide on the Internet. More than 1.7 million people "hit" the site, many of them journalists who wrote numerous articles about the David vs. Goliath battle.

There are many more examples of Internet damage. My point here is that you must be aware of what is being said about your organization. You could surf the Net yourself (or have an assistant do it) so you are aware of any rumors or allegations that are out there. If your company has high visibility generally, or if something is happening that suddenly makes you vulnerable to this type of attack, you may want to contract with a firm who makes it their business to monitor the Internet.

Another word of advice: talk to your organization's Webmaster. Be sure that there is a portion of your site which can be activated quickly to combat the misinformation. People will expect you to post the organization's side of the story, and you don't want to have to wait until the technical staff comes in to the office to set it up for you.

Crisis Prevention

One of my goals in writing this book and conducting the workshops is to get people in positions of authority to think seriously about crisis prevention. This is one case where an ounce of prevention really IS worth a pound of cure!

Managers and executives spend a great deal of time planning how to prevent sudden emergencies. Many manhours and lots of capital equipment are devoted to preventing accidents.

But it is also a good idea to invest some time and effort in preventing "creeping crises." Do you personally make it clear throughout your organization that acts of discrimination or harassment will not be tolerated? Do you need to revise (or write!) any policies? Should you train (or retrain) your supervisory personnel on how to respond when they receive an initial complaint?

You should give some serious thought to avoiding dumb decisions as well. Plenty of executives will tell you they wish they had spent more time thinking about the long-term consequences of some decisions before it was too late. Once you realize that an earlier decision put you on the wrong path, don't figure you have to continue on that path while your troubles mount. An old Turkish proverb says, "No matter how far you have gone down a wrong road, turn back."

Finally, be aware of what is being said about you on the Web. Otherwise, you could be blindsided by a crisis you didn't know was brewing. By then you will have lost your ability to manage the crisis.

The Value of a Clippings Binder

Whether you work for a private company, a governmental body, or any other organization, I highly recommend that you keep a clippings binder. Call it a scrapbook if you will. Just get a three-ring notebook and fill it with page protectors. Every time your organization is mentioned in the print media—trade magazine daily/weekly newspaper, newsletter, etc.—clip it and file it away. Doing it chronologically is easiest. Include the "good news" pieces: new hires/products, promotions, celebrations, awards, community projects, etc. Obviously, include pieces written about any crisis or controversial issue as well.

Such collections can come in very handy. Having a written history provides an accurate reminder when memory fails of exactly what was said publicly by you and about you. You can see which reporters have particular biases before you grant an interview. During periods of calm, it can remind you of how fragile that peace can be. In turbulent times, it will provide needed perspective—you've survived tough times before and you'll probably have more good times to come.

"Failing to prepare is preparing to fail."

John Wooden
Famed Basketball Coach, UCLA

4

The Value of a
Crisis Communications Plan

A crisis communications plan is not an emergency operational plan or a business continuity plan. Of course organizations need to have these. The chemical industry has Spill Control plans. Nursing homes have specific procedures to follow if a patient is missing. Utilities do certain things when part of their service area experiences a blackout.

What I am talking about here is a crisis *communications* plan. (See Figure 3, next page.) This details who should be notified in case of various types of crises. It may well be a different set of people, depending on the nature of the crisis. One thing for sure—it is **always** better to work this out in a non-crisis atmosphere when you can think clearly. Don't leave this up to one individual. Hold a meeting that involves several key people who can see the issues from various perspectives.

Who Needs to be Notified?

Figure out, before it happens, who in your organization needs to be notified about each type of problem. Does corporate want to be notified in cases of all problems that might become a crisis? Better to find out now rather than after the fact!

Figure 3

CRISIS COMMUNICATIONS PLAN

Note: Use separate sheet for each vulnerability

Vulnerability	Those to be Notified (with back-ups)	Contact Numbers	Action Steps
		Office Phone:	
		Home Phone:	
		Car Phone:	
		Cell Phone:	
		Pager:	
		Fax:	
		Office Phone:	
		Home Phone:	
		Car Phone:	
		Cell Phone:	
		Pager:	
		Fax:	
		Office Phone:	
		Home Phone:	
		Car Phone:	
		Cell Phone:	
		Pager:	
		Fax:	

Company Personnel

If it's an allegation of age/race/sexual discrimination, sexual harassment, or a labor dispute, you need your Human Resources expert. If it's a technical operational incident, you'll probably need Operations and Engineering personnel. In many instances, you'll need a Health, Safety and Environment expert to give you advice. If there are allegations of financial improprieties, you'll want to call on your Chief Financial Officer. And in many cases, you'll need to contact your legal counsel.

Non-Company Personnel

With regard to non-company personnel, it may be a good idea to talk to the individuals directly. Does the local Mayor of the small village in which you are located want to be awakened at 3 a.m. if your company experiences operational difficulties that could be noticed (flames, odors, loud noises) by some of his constituents? Or would he rather be contacted the next morning? If you wait until an incident occurs before you check on this, chances are good that you'll guess wrong and he'll be mad at you. (You are liable to find out just *how* mad the next time you go for a permit renewal or request an expansion of your operations!) Does the local Fire Chief want to be notified directly if you've had to activate your internal Plant Emergency Organization, just in case things get out of hand? Or does he want you to go through the full Mutual Aid notification drill? Check with the Fire Department and find out if they always want to be called even if the plant is handling an emergency. Find out ahead of time whom they will notify and whom they expect you to notify.

When you are thinking about whom to notify, don't forget that **you** may want to be the one to contact the media. If it's a public health issue, it is your moral and ethical responsibility to go beyond the strict legal requirements. Beyond that, though, it is often much better for your organization if you are the one to notify the media of a problem. If they find out about it over the emergency scanner or through their other sources, they will make their own decision on whether it is a big story and then approach you with a preconceived notion. Their first thought is likely to be that you were trying to hide something.

What Does a Communications Plan Look Like?

The format for this crisis communications plan need not be complex. It can be as simple as shown in Figure 3.

Remember that brainstorming you did in Chapter 1 where you listed what could go wrong in your organization that might bring the media to your door or unhappy people to a meeting? List down the far left column all the things you came up with: accident, fire, product recall, serious regulatory violation, bomb threat, violence in the workplace, missing patient, loss of accreditation, etc.

In the second column, list all of the people who should be notified in each event. Be sure you make provisions for one, or preferably two, back-ups in case the person you need is not available.

In the third column, record **all** of the phone/pager numbers where people can be reached—office, home, cell phone, e-mail, etc. Include fax numbers where appropriate.

Use the last column to lay out the initial steps that should be taken. You don't need to repeat the steps listed in your emergency operations plan. You can simply refer to it. However, if there has been a fatality in the workplace, for example, this would be the place to remind yourself that you need to:

- notify the local authorities;
- dispatch someone appropriate to personally break the news in as sensitive a way as possible before family members hear it on the radio or TV;
- notify the regulatory agencies;
- call in professionals who can provide grief counseling.

The Need for Speed

Of one thing you can be sure: in a crisis, people almost always feel that they were not notified soon enough or kept up to date. You have a thousand things to do. Making phone calls to all those who should be notified is a time-consuming process. You are likely to forget one or more people who will resent that fact. Sure, you can assign people to phone duty who are not immediately involved with trying to mitigate the incident. Even if you've been clear in your crisis communications plan who should be contacted, if there are a lot of people on this list, the last ones to be called are apt to be upset with you.

A solution that we found worked well for us in our company was to contract with a computerized emergency notification system known as the Community Alert Network (CAN). Simply by placing one telephone call to CAN headquarters, using a predetermined password to prove our identity, and recording a message with their operations personnel, our employees could quickly get back to solving the problem. They knew that the message was being transmitted so that all the people on our "need to know" list were contacted within just a few minutes and could begin to take the appropriate action.

At our company, we had pre-arranged to have on our CAN list some 80 key people—both employees and those in the surrounding community—who should be activated or who needed to be informed of what was happening. Other organizations arrange for certain areas to be notified based on their zip code. If a plume of hazardous material were released, just certain sectors of a large city can be called, depending on the wind direction. Communities where there might be a water main break, a lost child, a wandering Alzheimer's patient, or an escaped convict/mental patient could be alerted.

The families of all employees who were not hurt in an industrial accident could be notified they need not worry. One of my clients had this happen to them. Townspeople either heard the explosion or heard about the incident over the news. Their frantic phone calls to the plant overwhelmed the company's phone lines and prevented them from being able to make necessary outgoing emergency calls. I subsequently recommended that they subscribe to CAN.

With over 250 telephone lines available, CAN can make 15,000 calls in an hour. Recently a school district customer was able to contact 935 parents inside of 10 minutes to inform them of an incident at the school.

If you want to find out more about this highly effective means of speedy notification, call 1-800-848-3907 PIN 2145.

The Value of a Crisis Communications Plan

It is difficult to overstate the value of having an effective Crisis Communications Plan. The time you and your management team spend putting this together will be repaid many times over when you are called upon to use it. Time is something that is in very short supply when a crisis breaks. Being able to refer to this plan and start doing the right things immediately will save you a tremendous amount of pain and aggravation down the road. Without such a plan, you can quickly lose control while you decide who needs to be called, look up their phone numbers, and try to figure out what to do when the person you want doesn't answer the phone.

Those who are looking to see how you respond to this crisis will not be impressed if you are stumbling all over yourself. Such incompetence will leave them wondering if they should trust you to run the organization. Conversely, an organization that quickly implements a well thought-out crisis communications plan has a chance to take advantage of a limited window of opportunity.

A good example of this occurred in January of 1998 in the skiing industry. You may remember that, within five days of each other, both Sonny Bono and Michael Kennedy were killed in skiing accidents. The natural tendency of the media might have been to raise fears about the declining safety of the sport. Taken to an extreme, this could have severely impacted the industry.

What prevented that from happening? The National Ski Areas Association (NSAA) had a crisis plan developed that they could immediately implement. Part of that plan included the compilation of statistics that proved that the accident rate continued to average 36 fatalities a year for the past couple of years.

Within two hours after the first reports of Kennedy's death, the Association faxed nine pages of information to the media and to their member ski resorts. This allowed those resorts to respond properly to local media inquiries with consistent information. They also were able to quickly get in touch with a Ph.D. at the Rochester Institute of Technology who had studied ski injuries for 30 years. He was offered to the media as an objective authority on the subject.

What saved the NSAA from seeing these two tragic accidents spiral into an industry-wide crisis was the fact that they had a crisis plan ready. Right after the accident, they did not have to create a plan, look up the statistics, try to find an authoritative third-party source and figure out how to contact that person. The message that ended up being communicated was that skiing was a relatively safe sport if the skiers followed basic safety practices.

Two Very Important Reminders

(1) You **must** frequently review your crisis communications plan. Revise it regularly to reflect changes in the organization and its personnel. Double check phone/pager numbers. It is amazing how often they change.

(2) You must also periodically **drill** this plan. If not tested in a year, it is not reliable. You may have forgotten something or someone or discover that things that looked good on paper just don't work. Better to find out in a practice drill than when it really hits the fan!

If tempted to avoid putting together a simple crisis communications plan, think about this: how many **more** hours will be wasted (and productivity lost) while you run to play catch-up afterwards because the crisis lasted longer and got you in deeper trouble?

This point was dramatically proven on September 11, 2001 when the World Trade Center Towers in New York City were attacked. Through their shock and horror, residents of the metropolitan area were comforted and amazed at the way Mayor Rudy Giuliani was able to lead the city through its darkest days. Within two weeks, when the Mayor was a guest on David Letterman's late night TV show, Dave asked, "How IS it that you seemed to know all of the right things to do in the face of this overwhelming disaster?" The Mayor replied: "Dave, we DRILL on these things." He did not mean they drilled on having the two towers collapse, killing almost 3,000 people. But the City had an emergency plan that provided the framework upon which they could build. They were not starting from scratch, trying to remember what to do. They were implementing a plan.

II

Organizing to Handle a Crisis Effectively

It has been said that an organization needs to gain control of a crisis in the first 1-2 hours or they will spend the rest of their time chasing it. Long before a crisis of any type erupts, the wise organization has developed a plan and put a basic structure in place that will allow them to hit the ground running.

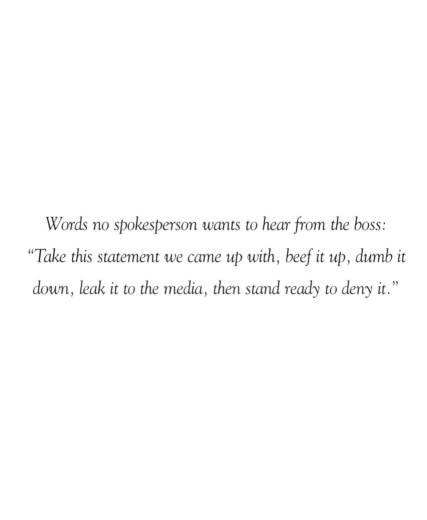

Words no spokesperson wants to hear from the boss:
"Take this statement we came up with, beef it up, dumb it
down, leak it to the media, then stand ready to deny it."

Identifying a Spokesperson

Author's Note: Throughout the rest of this book, I will need to refer to people who hold certain positions according to one gender or the other. I don't want to annoy you with constant he/she or her/his references, so I've made some arbitrary decisions I want to explain here.

I will refer to corporate CEO's, chief municipal government officials, plant managers and the other high-ranking people in the masculine. I know many terrific women who fill these top roles, but they are among the first to realize that they are still in the minority, and I trust that they will understand.

I will refer to the company spokesperson in the feminine. This is more or less a matter of convenience for me. It was the role which I filled when employed by a chemical manufacturing company. Obviously, many spokespersons are male. However, there are often good reasons why women are asked to fill this role. First, many male reporters state that they hesitate a little more to get aggressive or nasty with a woman. Secondly, women are often viewed by the public as more empathetic. We will discuss the great importance of empathy later. Third, my personal observation is that women often find it easier to say the two words, "I'm sorry," words frequently called for in a crisis.

CEO's might want to consider these things before they designate a spokesperson. Obviously, the overriding concern should be who has the best qualifications for this important job—something we will discuss in the next chapter.

Every organization should make it a part of its written policies that all media inquiries are directed to a previously identified spokesperson. Otherwise, you leave yourself open to the possibility that *any* employee could provide a statement to the media. It could be your most loyal and capable employee, or it could be the one recently disciplined for unsatisfactory performance.

Such a policy does not "forbid" employees from speaking to the press. You really don't want an employee to tell a reporter, "I'm not allowed to talk to you." Your company policy (written and communicated to everyone) should simply provide an agreed-upon procedure whereby employees can deflect questions to someone with this official responsibility. They are usually happy to do that.

Why Is the Spokesperson Not Always the CEO?

Many organizations assume the spokesperson always has to be the highest-ranking official. It is true that, in the case of a serious crisis, the media will eventually need to hear from the CEO. However, it is usually wise to identify someone else as the initial spokesperson. Here are three good reasons:

(1) *It saves the CEO time and aggravation.* Many questions from the press are routine. The CEO has more important things competing for his attention and he should not be distracted by having to respond to routine questions.

(2) *It automatically signals that the organization places more importance on the issues the CEO **does** comment on.* If the CEO has been answering questions about what the company does for its

employees around the holidays, for example, it will detract from the emphasis desired when the CEO comments on a serious incident.

(3) *It provides the CEO with a needed buffer.* This is critical. The initial spokesperson takes all incoming media inquiries and answers them whenever she is confident she knows the company position. When there is a crisis and the issue warrants a statement from the CEO, having the initial spokesperson as the first media contact will provide the CEO with valuable time. He can spend it—whether a few minutes or a few hours—developing a well thought out statement with a group of managers (called the Crisis Management Team, which will be discussed in the next chapter). If the CEO spoke directly to the media in the first moments of a crisis, he might give comments "off the top of his head," which could cause problems later.

Who Should Be Your Initial Spokesperson?

Your initial spokesperson fulfills a very important role. If your organization has a competent communications/public relations professional on staff, your choice should be obvious.

Smaller organizations often have to look throughout their workforce (senior or middle managers, health/safety/environmental professionals or administrative assistants, etc.) for someone who has as many as possible of the following characteristics:

(1) *Accessibility*: The media has to be able to get to the spokesperson readily. Choosing someone with a heavy travel schedule does not make much sense.

(2) *Willingness*: You are not doing your employee or your organization any favors by appointing someone who is terrified at the prospect of doing this job. (However, neither do you want some-

one who is **too** willing to see her face on camera or her name in print!)

(3) *Coachability*: The person cannot be so headstrong as to say whatever she has decided is right, regardless of the guidance and direction provided by the Crisis Management Team. No room for loose cannons here.

(4) *Assertiveness*: However, the spokesperson cannot be a doormat either. If she realizes that management is not providing the community with the information that the public wants and needs, she has to have the confidence to bring this to their attention. Bucking the rest of the management team can be a little tricky, so it takes someone with tact, self-confidence, and trust in her instincts.

(5) *Appropriate demeanor*: The organization should be proud of its spokesperson. Management should choose someone who looks and acts professionally, conveys sincerity, and is generally a nice person. Putting someone in this position who lacks interpersonal skills or who loses her temper easily is an invitation to disaster.

(6) *Ability to act calm*: Although it is difficult to **be** calm in a crisis, it is important to choose someone who can **act** calm. You want to convey that the company is effectively handling the situation. If the spokesperson appears on camera wild-eyed and frantic, it will not convey the proper message. It helps if the spokesperson has had experience with crises before and knows that, if the crisis is handled professionally, the organization will survive. As my grandmother often said, "This too shall pass." An ability to maintain perspective is important.

(7) *Facility with written and spoken language*: It is critical that this person be able to take notes on management's comments in a Crisis Management Team meeting and, once back at her desk,

quickly put together a clear, logical statement. Someone who gets frequent writer's block will not succeed, especially since there is NEVER enough time in a crisis. Reporters rarely will just accept the company's written statement, so the spokesperson must be able to think on her feet. She has to be able to answer follow-up questions clearly and concisely.

(8) *Knowledge of your business*: A spokesperson does not need to understand all of the technical aspects of your business. However, she **must** be able to answer basic questions about your organization, its products/services, history, normal methods of operating, and its place in the community. If every question the media asks is met with "I don't know, but I'll get back to you on that," reporters will quickly lose patience, and your organization will lose credibility. Certainly, the spokesperson cannot be expected to know the answer to all questions. That's where you bring in your subject matter experts.

If both your CEO and your initial spokesperson display all of these characteristics, LUCKY YOU! Most organizations have to choose people who fit most of these characteristics and then train to fill the gaps.

You Must Also Identify Back-Ups!

Now that you are happy to have found two people who can fulfill these roles, you need to identify at least two more! Murphy's Law is always in effect. The day you have a crisis, your CEO will be in Europe on business and your spokesperson will be camping in the wilderness or have the flu and laryngitis.

Everyone in the organization, particularly the receptionists, security guards or anyone who usually answers the phones, needs to know who to turn to as the initial spokesperson and as the alternates. It is important to provide media training to all of these folks and to your subject matter experts as well. You don't want them to inadvertently stumble into major problems and undo all of the solid media and community relations work you have been doing.

Choosing your spokesperson is one of the most important decisions you will make. It must be done carefully, taking into consideration all of the above. Handling a crisis is difficult enough as it is. Not being confident that you have the best possible person on the "front lines" will make things even harder and can possibly even lengthen the crisis for you.

6

Assembling Your Crisis Management Team (CMT)

(Note: For those readers in the emergency services, the CMT is equivalent to the "Command" Section of the Incident Command System.)

No one person should have to deal with a crisis alone. You want a limited number of people speaking to the press, but behind the scenes, exemplary teamwork is required. An organization needs to respond quickly or the crisis will take control of them, placing them on the defensive and making them look incompetent or insensitive to the needs of the public—or both.

Speedy response requires selecting ahead of time who should be on your Crisis Management Team (CMT). (Remember, you should have done this when you were developing that Crisis Communications Plan described in Chapter 4.) The first person informed of the crisis must know right away who needs to be contacted and must be confident of having all current phone/beeper/pager numbers. I strongly recommend to my clients that they always carry with them a laminated wallet-sized card with the day and night contact numbers of all those who might be called upon as CMT members.

Who Are the Core Members of the CMT?

In almost every case, the highest-ranking official should lead this group. Whenever he is unavailable for more than a day, he should designate a replacement. In a crisis, this will preclude wasting time caused by people jockeying for position. In those rare cases where it is recognized that the CEO does not function well in crisis situations, he should be put in charge of running normal operations and receive regular briefings on the crisis.

Other core members of most CMT's include:

- *The Director of Human Resources.* Many crises are directly related to their area of expertise: employee lawsuits, labor issues, or hiring/firing of people. Even if the crisis does not immediately involve employees, your work force needs accurate information on what is happening. The Director of Human Resources is often in the best position to communicate with employees.

- *Legal Counsel.* Crises often have legal implications, so professional legal advice should be sought. The CEO must listen to this advice because lawyers are trying to protect the organization's rights. However, the CEO must also be aware that the natural tendency of legal counsel is to advise organizations not to say anything to the public, and this could be dangerous in terms of their corporate reputation.

    A whole book could be written on the differences between the court of law and the court of public opinion. Lawyers are trained to pay attention to the specifics of written laws and the precedents courts have set. It is all about logic and rules. There are strict boundaries about what is allowed.

    When dealing with the court of public opinion, on the other hand, there are no boundaries. There are no rules. Everything is given equal weight: truth, rumors, lies, and misinterpretations.

Many progressive organizations believe that the unfavorable publicity they would receive for taking a strictly legalistic approach to their crisis would be far worse than losing or settling any lawsuit. Maybe they have also heard what I've been told. When lawsuits DO arise, judges and juries are often much less apt to "throw the book" at an organization which has shown some compassion and a willingness to apologize and make amends.

In our lawsuit-happy society, chances are good that someone will try to sue the organization if something has gone wrong. P.R. people advise reaching out and the lawyers advise keeping quiet. The decision falls squarely in the lap of the CEO. How can he strike a balance between the legal advice and his moral and ethical responsibility to be responsive to the needs of the public, including the media? He needs to weigh the disadvantages of possibly saying something wrong early in the crisis against the benefits of being perceived as straightforward, credible and concerned about the situation.

My point here is to have these discussions around the CMT table. Too often organizations work hard to develop a statement. Then, just before they are ready to deliver it, their legal counsel advises—in the sternest of tones—that they should not say anything. This throws everything into an uproar and makes it impossible for the organization to move quickly.

- *The Spokesperson.* The final member of the core CMT should be the designated initial spokesperson. Many times, this individual has had special training in public relations and media affairs. The CMT cannot develop a position statement without her if they expect her to act intelligently as the liaison to the media. Reporters will inevitably want comments beyond the printed statement. If the spokesperson has not been privy to the discussions around the CMT table, she will not be able to handle the follow-up questions effectively. Some of the most disastrous media interviews can be traced to the fact that the spokesperson was not brought into the "inner circle" while various strategies, approaches and options were being considered.

Who Else is Added to the Core CMT?

Depending on the nature of the crisis, other senior managers and support personnel should join the CMT. In a product liability issue, you would need the Marketing Manager. In an operational issue, you would call upon the Production Director. A hostile takeover bid or accusations of financial impropriety would require the Chief Financial Officer. Issues with important safety or environmental aspects would require employees with special expertise in these areas. Municipal heads should be able to call on emergency management professionals or experts in water, traffic, safety or law enforcement. (Please remember that the company has to identify at least one back-up person in each of these areas in case the primary person is out of town or ill.)

The CMT should then identify any others who have special knowledge about different kinds of problems. Who knows the most about a particular product, process or procedure? Who has the best relationship with affected customers? Who has the closest ties and most credibility with elected officials or regulators? These people can either be added to the CMT or put on alert that their services may be needed.

Remember that speedy mobilization of the CMT is required if you are to get off to a decent start. The only way this can be done effectively is if you have thought through, in calmer times, who should be on the CMT and notified them of that fact. In the next chapter, we will discuss what the CMT does when a crisis strikes.

7

Putting Your
CMT to Work

Acrisis has erupted and the media has gotten wind of it. The phones are ringing off the hook or members of the press are showing up at your door. You have contacted the members of the Crisis Management Team (CMT). How do you organize yourselves to be the most effective?

The CMT meets together in a pre-determined place.

Now is not the time for people to be wandering around trying to find each other. You should pre-establish in which office, conference room or cubicle you will meet. Identify a secondary site in case that spot is not available, perhaps because it is too close to the incident.

Place trusted employees at the front desk and/or on the switchboard.

Many organizations have replaced their smiling front desk receptionists with automated attendants. Personally, I think that is a shame. In daily interactions with companies, most of us would rather deal with a human being, whether as you walk through the front door or when you call the general number on the telephone. I am aware that I am fighting a losing battle here as many organizations have opted for the cost savings associated with automation.

However, you must be aware that, during a crisis, you NEED competent human beings at the front desk/security office to answer calls from the public and the media. You don't want these callers lost in Voice Mail Hell. Neither do you want any people who may show up in your lobby (whether the media or others) to simply wander into your offices or other areas of your facility. Employees who might be called upon to staff the switchboard or front desk positions should be trained beforehand. They need to know how to handle incoming inquiries properly, directing them to the right person or showing them where to wait until someone can help them. They also should receive training in how to handle angry/upset people.

Establish a separate area as the Media Center.

Make sure the members of the press corps are comfortable. Have coffee/soda and food available, especially if the incident is apt to take some time to resolve. Reporters may still need access to phones, computer hook-ups and fax machines. They should be assured that staying in this Media Center provides them with the best chance of getting the most current information. You do not want them wandering around.

The facility manager should notify upper management or regional offices that an incident is occurring.

These folks do not like hearing news like this from the media. They may be able to provide additional resources such as public affairs or legal counsel.

Begin gathering the facts about the incident as soon as possible.

Find out as much as you can about exactly what has happened. Try to get information from several sources. You do not want to be locked into one individual's reporting bias or tendency to shade the facts to cover themselves or their people.

A "position log" should be kept. Having precise notes as you move through the crisis about who did what when will become very important later on. You cannot depend on people's memories. Noting the exact times when various things occurred, when certain responses were made and who told what to whom may play an important part in helping you assess your crisis response, provide information to insurance carriers, facilitate reimbursement, etc.

Analyze the situation.

The members of the CMT should first determine if there is anything that must be communicated to others immediately because of health or safety concerns. If not, you have more time to determine what should be done. Do not limit your work to simply conveying the facts.

Analyzing what has happened and what needs to be done next is where the real work of crisis response is done, and the skills of many different people will be called upon here.

In the area of crisis communications that is my area of expertise, you want to be thinking about things like:

- Is there a root cause that must be ferreted out?
- Did the crisis point out a weakness in your organization's policies, procedures, or processes?
- Are there improvements that should be made to help prevent a recurrence?

These are all items which it will be important to communicate at the appropriate time.

Think through the questions you are most likely to be asked.

You dare not go to an interview without having spent some quality time doing this. Put yourself in the shoes of the public. It almost goes without saying that you should be as prepared as possible to answer the basic questions every reporter is trained to ask: the 5 W's and an H (who, what, where, when, why, and how). But go beyond that. What else will they want to know?

Try your answers out on the members of your CMT until they sound right. Then test them on administrative or clerical staff who are not as involved in the technicalities as are those on the CMT. Do they understand what you are trying to say?

When you are satisfied that you have good answers for these questions, practice them until you know them well. (A more detailed discussion of preparing for tough questions can be found in Chapter 18.)

Develop the key messages you wish to communicate.

What do you most want the public to understand and remember? People are able to recall only three or four things, even about a crisis situation. Make sure you work on stating these key messages (or "must air" messages) in simple, clear words. Describe the situation so folks can readily understand. Illustrate or explain your points in memorable ways, if possible. (More details about these subjects will be found in Chapters 19 and 20.)

Provide the information to your various audiences.

This part requires some clear thinking as to whom you notify first. It really depends on the particular situation. (Now is another good time to refer to that Crisis Communications Plan from Chapter 4.)

If it is an issue of public health and safety, you have to notify the media quickly to enlist their help in spreading the word. If an evacuation is required, this can only be ordered by the responsible government authority for your area. If employees are injured, a major responsibility is to reach out personally to their families and then to the rest of the employees. Each member of the CMT should be directed to communicate the key messages to a given audience—the one with whom they have the best rapport. For instance, the facility manager might contact corporate and the local elected officials (who never want to tell a constituent they don't know the answer to a question). The Human Resources Director uses whatever methods are available (bulletin board, e-mail, videoconferencing, word-of-mouth through supervisors) to inform employees what is happening. Their livelihoods may be at stake, so they have an intense desire—and a right—to know. The spokesperson meets with the assembled media to provide a preliminary briefing and a promise to return at regular intervals to update them. Your Health, Safety and Environmental Director could notify the appropriate regulatory officials. (Even if regulatory reporting is not required to preclude fines, they will probably appreciate hearing from you directly before someone else questions them.)

Go back and repeat steps from the fact-gathering stage until the situation is resolved.

In most crises, you will go through these steps of the process several times as new facts become known. As long as you provide accurate and timely information, there is less likelihood that reporters will search for other sources of information and/or be angry with you about not cooperating with them.

Crises are, by their nature, stressful. An organization that takes all of these steps is on the right track. Following this advice will not eliminate the stress, but it will help organize the chaos to a point where it can be better dealt with for all concerned.

Think carefully about who you are really talking to in a crisis. Then recognize your messages will be heard or read by your employees, your competitors, your friends and your critics all at the same time. Challenging, isn't it?

SECTION

III

Understanding Your Audiences

Before opening your mouth to speak, you need to have a clear understanding of those to whom you are speaking through the media. Who are they? What do they think about you? What is on their minds? What is important to them? Spend some time thinking through the answers to these questions to save yourself a lot of trouble during a crisis.

Carefully consider who will think they should be informed about the crisis and prepare to give them the information they need. This way they can become your allies, not your enemies.

8

Identifying Your Audiences

W hen something goes wrong at your organization, a LOT of people will be interested. They will want to know what has happened, why it happened, and what you are doing to remedy the situation. Most people don't like stress in their lives, so they will be anxious to know what you are doing to bring life back to normal. Who are the people with whom you need to be communicating?

Obviously, if there is a public health/safety emergency—a severe weather alert, an accidental chemical release, a fire, explosion, or contaminated food, for example—you absolutely need to get to the general public immediately. This will probably be done through the media, unless you have a system like CAN (see pages 23-24). As quickly as you can, you must tell those who might be affected what to do to protect the health and safety of themselves and their families. However, if the crisis is not so urgent, I recommend you consider another order of notification.

Your Employees

Yes, I have put them first. In actual practice, many times they are the last people to be told what is going on. Consider the following scenario. One of your employees is approached at a community event:

"Hey, John! You work down there at Acme Manufacturing, right? What's the scoop on all this stuff I've been reading in the newspaper about them this past week? Sounds to me like those people you work for haven't been acting responsibly and are now trying to cover it up! What's going on?"

Imagine this answer from your employee: "What do you want from me, Joe? I don't know from nothin'. They don't tell us a thing. Just expect us to go to work every day, run ourselves ragged working all kinds of overtime so we're dead on our feet, and then send us home. They're too busy, they tell us, to take time out for employee meetings to fill us in on what's really going on. What does the newspaper say?"

OOPS! Now imagine this conversation duplicated many times over in different parts of town with different employees, some of whom might be even more upset with the company than the poor, tired guy above.

At best, this exchange demonstrates a major lost opportunity to spread accurate information, thereby counteracting rumor, innuendo, and inaccurate reporting. At worst, such conversations can lead to an increasingly negative impression about your organization. Neighbors would likely expect employees to know what was going on, especially if there were negative media stories appearing about their employer.

Consider the far different result if the employee had been prepared to answer like this: "You know, Joe, it's been very upsetting to all of us at Acme to see the way the newspapers have been reporting about this situation. The president of the company held a series of meetings for all of us last week just so he could tell us what is really going on. If all you know is what you read in the papers, you would really get the wrong impression about our company. I'm convinced that we are trying to do the right thing. It's a bit complicated, but here's what I understand is happening..."

What a world of difference! By taking the time to tell the employees what is going on, the company now has vastly expanded its public relations staff. Your employees have a great deal of credibility in their community. People are more apt to believe the guy next door than the "official line" provided by the Public Affairs Officer or even the CEO.

So, use this to your advantage! Get everyone together in a face-to-face meeting where they can get answers to their own questions (the BEST communications tool). If you can't do that, or do it quickly, at least post the facts and the company position on bulletin boards or the internal computer network. Establish a rumor hot line where employees can check things out. Make sure your supervisors are well briefed so they can answer questions from those who report to them. Use whatever channels of communication work best in your company to keep your employees informed. They can be a big help in difficult situations.

Local Elected Officials

Mentioned before, it bears repeating. Corporations must keep elected officials apprised of crisis situations. For simplicity's sake I'll refer to these folks as "the Mayor" here, but it applies to officials at all levels (village, town, city, state—even federal, if needed).

There are two very good reasons to keep these folks well informed, especially during a crisis.

(1) I have never yet met one elected official who wanted to reply to a constituent's question with the words "I don't know." They

want to be able to appear informed, involved, and on top of things. If they have to admit they don't know something—especially about a situation that is prompting concern within their jurisdiction—the result will not be pleasant for you. The elected official may assume the worst and start making public negative statements that he will later find hard to retract.

Failing to notify the appropriate officials could result in receiving an angry phone call—or worse. After you have worked hard to develop a good relationship with the officials in your community relations outreach efforts, you don't want this sort of setback. What can you possibly say when he yells at you for not telling him sooner? You didn't remember him? You didn't think he'd want to know? He'll be annoyed or insulted or both.

If you had previously worked on establishing a good rapport, you may be forgiven for this initial oversight during a crisis. (But don't let it happen again!) But if it is a repeat offense or the Mayor and municipal board are angry enough, your next appearance before them might be a lot more difficult. That permit for a facility expansion could be delayed or even denied. You may find special permit conditions added to your operating agreements. Or you may find the municipal Building Code Enforcement officer making more frequent visits. You get the picture.

In government circles, remember that those above you have needed resources and you want to maintain a good relationship.

(2) It is simply human nature that people are most influenced by what they hear first. It creeps into their brain and becomes the story. All subsequent information is bounced off of it. If the first story the Mayor and Board members hear is that something you

have done has placed the public safety in jeopardy or is morally or ethically unsavory, you will have to work hard to erase that negative first impression. Try hard to be the one who shapes the story in the minds of elected officials. Believe me, when a reporter gets around to contacting the Mayor for his take on the situation, you will be GLAD you did!

Regulatory Officials

I am going to assume here that you will, without a doubt, notify the appropriate agencies if you are required to do so by law. But there are other situations where it may not be immediately clear if a regulation has been violated. My advice: re-read the above section on elected officials. Much of what was said there applies to those in positions of authority in the regulatory agencies, whether they are in charge of protecting the environment or regulating nursing homes, banks, hospitals, utilities, etc.

I know your blood runs cold at the thought of alerting these folks to situations they might not absolutely need to know about. You fear that you will get a black mark on your record when it might not be legally necessary. You know that it is possible that they will overreact and make a big deal out of something that does not warrant it.

There are several good reasons to at least consider my advice. The most important is this: it is likely that they will hear about the situation some other way. Concerned citizens call agencies to report things that upset them. Local offices of these agencies read regional newspapers.

Wouldn't you much rather reach out to the regulators first with a "heads up" phone call? "I don't believe we will be required to report what happened tonight, but there are some concerns we are dealing with among our neighbors, so we thought you would like to know." That outreach could go a long way toward improving your relationship with agency officials and enhancing your credibility.

Emergency Responders

In most towns across the country, the opinion of the Fire Chief or the Police Chief is the most respected. These emergency responders are not subject to the negatives often associated with "politicians."

If you can get the Chief to speak up during a time of crisis with a reassuring word to the public, you will go a long way toward solving the problem. He will be viewed as an objective third party whose primary concern is protecting the public. If he steps before the TV camera and says, "We are working closely with company officials and feel certain that we will have this situation under control in the next hour with no further threat to the local citizens," you are in good shape. If he is interviewed before you have had a chance to brief him, the message will be a lot less positive. "We don't know what's going on inside the facility yet" will only promote fear and possibly panic.

The Media

The media is a major audience during a crisis. In an operational incident, in many cases, they heard about it at the same time or before you did. They may be waiting for you with microphones in hand when you arrive, telling you about their deadlines. You may not like to see them there, but you have to realize they have an important job to do and deal with them accordingly.

A new twist to media access was added in 2002. In California, a law now requires media representatives be given access to emergency sites (except crime scenes) after being warned it might be dangerous. Emergency responders are struggling with all of this, including the fact that these folks could be listening to all of their conversations, etc. Some say this is crazy:

- They don't have hazardous materials training required of others on scene;
- Who judges whether a person who runs a web site is a legitimate media representative?
- Who will pay when the local TV intern trips on a fire hose and breaks an ankle and sues? (This has already happened!)

Whether this law will be rescinded or spread to other states remains to be seen, but it is something which should be taken into consideration.

If there is a health threat, the electronic media can be your greatest allies because they can reach the public quickly. Unless you have had the foresight to contract with an emergency dialing system that quickly notifies individual neighbors by delivering a specific emergency response message over the telephone (see details on the CAN system in Chapter 4), you must depend on TV and radio. They can broadcast special bulletins to augment the notification systems used by your local emergency responders. You need the media during a crisis like this. They need speedy and accurate information from you. You must work cooperatively.

In situations that do not involve an immediate health/safety emergency, you have a little more time. Think through the needs of the various types of media channels.

(1) Radio needs verbal sound bites—well thought out and concise, but informative. They have extremely short deadlines with news shows aired every half-hour (and they can air emergency bulletins any time). They want to be updated frequently so they can report the latest status as they go through a day's news reports.

(2) TV reporters need visuals—the more dramatic, the better. A burning building, an injured employee, a frightened mother holding a crying one-year old, panic-stricken family members of a missing mental patient–all this makes news footage. TV deadlines are usually a little more forgiving than radio unless the situation is big enough to break into normally scheduled programs with live coverage. You need to know if they have a News at Noon show or just evening productions (usually shown around 6 p.m. and repeated later several times).

They, too, want quotable quotes and concise explanations on camera. You should also give them additional information—a written statement—so they can be as accurate as possible in the anchor's introduction or closing of the piece. (The way you present your story—how you appear on camera—is vitally important here and will be dealt with in Chapters 24 and 25.)

(3) Print reporters have more opportunity to treat a story in depth, and they often are not on as short a deadline (unless your timing is very unfortunate). While they will look for clever ways to express the story, they have more time and space to provide background and context.

This means it is incumbent on you to have relevant information readily available for them. A press kit (more about the contents of that in Chapter 22) should be available.

Hopefully, you have already laid a lot of groundwork with the media before the crisis broke. A full discussion of Media Relations 101 must wait for another time. Here just let me mention a few key things. The reporters will know your reputation in dealing with the media as they arrive to cover this story. This can be to your advantage or your detriment.

Ideally, you will have invited the reporters in to your organization for a "backgrounder session" when there was no crisis, just to get to know each other and to familiarize them with your operations. If they see you as a decent human being (or even a "real nice guy") who is making every effort to competently run an operation that is ethical, safe, environmentally sound, and operated with the public interest paramount, it will set the tone for any future stories, even when a crisis has erupted.

It does no one any good to spend a lot of time "bashing" the media. There are good and bad examples of people in this profession just as there are in any other. Basically, you will find most journalists just want to do a good job and deliver an accurate story. They do have their own set of personal priorities, however, and it is a wise person who has taken the time to understand what they are. (See Chapter 9 for a further explanation of them.)

A practicing journalist once said a very perceptive thing about his profession. The job of a reporter is "to afflict the comfortable and comfort the afflicted." A great sound bite that describes the mindset of a lot of reporters! If you can see it from their point of view, you will be a lot better off.

The Public
These are the people you should be addressing through all of your comments to the media. They make up the audience you are trying to influence when you grant media interviews to radio, TV, or newspapers.

It is very important to understand that when you speak to a large group of people, **they will not all receive your message in the same way**. Their impression of what you say will depend on their previous knowledge and experience with you (or your industry in general) and what else is going on in their own lives. If you are with a hospital, and the person hearing about your current situation recently had a bad experience in your institution, he will be prepared to think the worst and believe everything your critics have to say about you. It is helpful to have some understanding of these different segments of society, so please look at Chapter 10: "The Difference Between Supporters and Splenetics."

Here I just want to mention that you should not limit your public outreach to those things that are communicated through the media. An internationally known crisis management expert, whom I am honored to also call a friend, Jim Lukaszewski, has written a great little book on this topic. It's a quick read—one medium-length airplane trip should do it. The title is *Influencing Public Attitudes: Strategies that Reduce the Media's Power*. In it, Jim says:

> "*Allowing the media to drive your strategy is a recipe for failure...Many situations do cause intense media interest to which you must respond. When your issues or problems...have a high profile among key audiences, it's in your best interests to discuss them and work them out...BUT if you've had contact with those groups who are most directly affected, media coverage simply becomes less and less relevant. You have reduced the media's power, yet built your own credibility.*"

What this means is that you must have an ongoing community outreach program. It need not be expensive or require a vast number of manhours. In my 16 years as the Manager of Public Affairs for a chemical manufacturing company, I spent a good deal of energy, time, and effort organizing community outreach activities that were carried out by a number of different people throughout the company. Many hands make for a light load.

Community relations could be the subject for an entire book.

Here is a brief summary of possible approaches. You might have an occasional Open House or a series of plant tours where you can show people who you are and what your organization does. Perhaps a few employees would be willing to go out to local service clubs, church groups and senior citizen organizations to show a video or slides and answer questions. Scientists, engineers, nurses, accountants, bank tellers, store managers, etc. may be willing to participate in Career Days at local schools.

One of the BEST means of reaching out to neighbors—especially in the aftermath of an incident that prompted concern among the public—is what Jim Lukaszewski calls "belly-button-to-belly-button communication." Your gut to their gut, so to speak—really getting in there and having a heart-to-heart talk about what happened, what the organization is doing about it, listening to them, answering their questions, and TRULY responding to their concerns. So now, when the media writes an article with a negative tone or inaccuracies, the public has factual information they can use to balance it. Besides, they have had a positive personal interaction with some nice person from your organization who took the time to explain the situation fully, and to care about their concerns. See how much it improves your odds?

If you would like to discuss community relations issues, programs or activities, a field in which I specialized for 17 years, feel free to contact me (see back page).

Again, I want to emphasize that the order in which you contact these various audiences may vary, depending on the situation. I just want you to *consider* them all. In some cases you may opt not to contact all of these audiences. Just make sure you have a good reason. Forget one or more of them in the heat of the battle, and you will probably live to regret it!

"Well, we've got to sell newspapers!"

—Any Reporter, Anytown, U.S.A.

9

Understanding a Journalist's Priorities

I t hardly ever fails. When I conduct a workshop, at least one of the participants wants to tell me about how badly he was once treated by the media. The reporter got it all wrong. He was misquoted. His remarks were taken out of context. His comments were misinterpreted. The reporter ignored the good news and concentrated on the bad. Usually this individual concludes by saying that he will never talk to the media, "because they only twist everything to fit their own purpose."

In most cases, I just don't buy this. Sure, I'll admit that reporters can get things wrong. In fact, this happened to me on more than one occasion when I was the spokesperson for a chemical manufacturer. However, there are several major reasons why this might happen, and we—the subjects of the story—usually bear at least some of the responsibility. Perhaps we were not as clear as we needed to be. We may not have given the reporter enough background on the situation. Or we didn't say things concisely enough for them to be able to use it without changing it.

Even if you do everything right, though, it is possible you will still end up on the short end of the stick. Usually this is not because the reporter is truly out to "get" you. (It must be said, however, that this *can* happen in rare cases. If this is true, you have a lot more work to do in the area of basic media relations.) In the majority of cases, when the story does not turn out the way you would have liked, it can be traced to the journalist's priorities. It is a wise individual who knows about these priorities if you plan to work with the media.

What is Important to Journalists?

Let's look at a survey conducted among journalists where they ranked what was important to them.

1. *Themselves*

At least they are honest about this. Their goal is to write a story that gets them noticed. They would like to win journalistic awards to advance their careers. They would love to be promoted to a better "beat" within their newspaper or be picked up by a newspaper (or a TV/radio station) with a larger audience.

Journalists do not get noticed by writing dull stories. They need to be dramatic. They may even consciously want to provoke controversy where there is none. If they can conduct some investigative reporting that uncovers corporate/municipal wrongdoing, what a coup!

2. *Their Bosses*

Meeting the expectations of their superiors is the only way reporters will be able to move along the accelerated career track they crave. Their bosses want excitement. If there is a hint of controversy, reporters are sorely tempted to puff it up to win the praise of those above them.

3. *Their Sources*

Here is a key point for all those who are the subject of stories (the "principals"). Just glance further in this chapter to see how far down the list the "principals" appear! (A hint: it doesn't go any lower!) So every story subject should strive to become a "source."

What does it mean to be a source? At the bigger newspapers, some reporters tend to specialize in a certain kind of story—health, environmental, hearth and home, etc. But the reporters assigned by the news desk editor and those who work for smaller publications have to write about a wide variety of topics. They cannot possibly know a lot about every subject they are assigned to cover. One day they cover a municipal board meeting on a development project and a fire at a warehouse; the next day they are asked to interview a local woman who won a state-wide cooking contest; the next they are told to uncover what went wrong when a hospital mixed up two babies and sent them home with the wrong mothers; then they must make sense out of a story about parts per million of a toxic substance found in the soil on a piece of land in the local village.

Because they cannot possibly be educated about all subjects, they have to depend on people whom they can trust to provide them with accurate and reliable information—their sources.

If you work on developing a relationship of mutual trust and respect with a reporter and help with background information whenever you have a chance, you may become a source. Reporters are very considerate of their sources. They cannot do without them. This does not mean they won't do a tough story on you if it is deserved. It does mean, however, that they are more apt to treat you fairly and even give you the benefit of the doubt on occasion.

This type of relationship is worth a great deal, so don't ever overlook your opportunity to move up the food chain!

4. *Their Peers*

Like most other people, journalists want the approval of their colleagues. Unusual approaches and dramatic stories may gain the respect of those with whom they work. It makes reporters feel good to impress their peers.

5. *Their Readers/Viewers*

Look how far down the list this audience is! When I was starting out in my position as media spokesperson for our chemical company, I was naively of the opinion that journalists wrote stories or produced TV news in order to educate, inform, and protect the public. And, in fact, many reporters will say this is why they chose the profession of journalism. But remember that this list of "Journalists' Priorities" was compiled from actual interviews with journalists themselves!

This was brought home forcefully to me one day in a conversation with a local newspaper reporter. She had written several stories about the dangers posed by a chemical residue found in the soil near our company's plant. Even though I repeatedly made the point to her about the very small parts per million of the substance she was writing about, she neglected to mention this in her stories. People in the community were becoming quite concerned. I could tell this from the increased number of phone calls I fielded and the numerous Letters to the Editor on the topic. So when I encountered the reporter in town one day, I asked: "Doesn't it bother you at all that you are unnecessarily alarming a lot of people in the community?" Without batting an eye, she came back with a sly smile and this comment: "Well, you know, we've got to sell newspapers!"

We may not like this answer, but we simply have to deal with it because it is true.

6. *The Principals*

That's you—the one the story is about. It does little good to rail against being on the bottom of the pile. It is simply the way it is.

Accept it and determine to make the best of it. Do what you can to make the reporter's job easy—give him accurate information that helps him tell the story in an interesting way. By doing so, you will gain the reporter's respect. With luck and a little hard work, you may even move up to position #3—being a source.

Before leaving this chapter, let me urge you again to do whatever you can during periods of calm to establish decent working relationships with the local media. Get to know the reporters who usually cover your organization, whether it be the City Desk for hard news (an accident), the healthcare reporter for hospitals, the local "stringer" who covers municipal meetings, the financial expert for banking stories, the education specialist, etc. Invite these folks to a "backgrounder" on your organization. Let them meet key people so they know you as nice folks. When it's time to write a controversial story, they won't view you as a faceless stranger. It can make a BIG difference!

My friend, Carolyn Harshman, who does a lot of training for municipalities and their emergency responders, provided a great example of how this can work: When San Diego County became aware that recent weather patterns made it highly likely that the area would experience difficult flooding in the spring, they put together a meeting where plans and preparations for this situation would be discussed. Carolyn wisely opted to issue personal invitations to representatives of <u>all</u> print and electronic media so that they could be better informed and meet those who would be their resources when the floods hit. The result? The subsequent coverage of the floods was factual and free of attempts to search for those who should have done a better job of preparing for it. The media actually seemed to compete for who could write the best story!

A lot of people are waiting to hear your side of the story in a crisis. Give them the facts, stated reasonably and with the interests of the public in mind, if you want to have a good chance for success.

CHAPTER

10

The Difference Between Supporters and Splenetics

In Chapter 8, I mentioned that one of the important audiences you must address when something has gone wrong is the public-at-large. This is not a homogeneous group. In fact, "the public" is extremely diverse. Your statements in the media will be heard or read simultaneously by:

- members of a vocal activist group that opposes you
- community residents/taxpayers
- your friends at the Rotary and Lions Clubs
- students and faculty members from the school your child attends
- your colleagues in neighboring businesses
- neighborhood groups
- your own employees, and
- possibly your shareholders.

But it gets even more complicated! Within each group, there may be a wide range of opinions about you and your organization. For example, within environmental activist groups, there are people who have legitimate concerns which they can discuss rationally. There are also members who are more emotional than reasoned, who have a personal agenda, or whose main purpose is to create controversy so they can raise money for the organization. Among the Rotarians, there may be an individual whose son you fired because he had unsafe work habits or fell asleep on the job. There may also be people who are grateful to the company because you have volunteered to be a speaker or donated to their scholarship fund.

When speaking in a public setting or being interviewed by the media, never assume that you know exactly where "the public" is coming from. I would prefer that you think about "the public" as individuals who fall somewhere along this bell curve shown in Figure 4. I refer to them as "the Five S's." Let's consider each group from left to right:

Figure 4

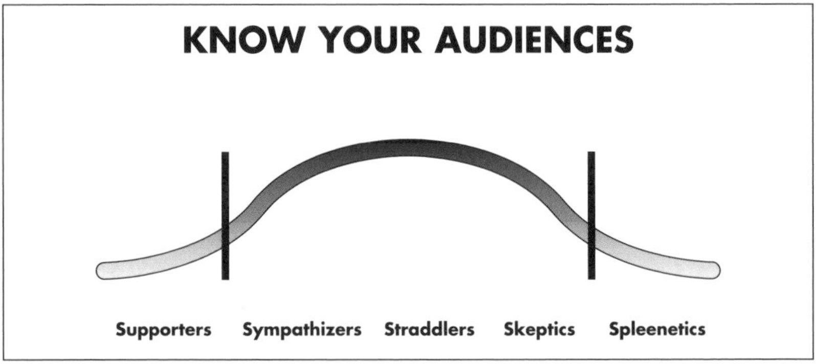

KNOW YOUR AUDIENCES

Supporters   Sympathizers   Straddlers   Skeptics   Spleenetics

Supporters

On the far left, a small group of people thinks your organization is great. There can be any number of reasons. Maybe you employ them or a member of their family. Perhaps you are a major customer for their business. They have benefited from dealings with your organization in the past. Perhaps your Fire Department successfully fought a fire at their house. Somehow they have come to the conclusion that yours is an honorable organization, worthy of trust.

These folks will not readily believe bad things that may be said about your organization. Someone will have to prove gross incompetence or misconduct or negligence for them to change their minds about you.

Sympathizers

To their right is a larger group of people. They have no particular reason to think badly of you. In fact, most of what they have heard about your organization has been fairly positive. They have known a few employees in the community who seem like good people; they serve together on boards of the local Little League or Red Cross. The school club their child belongs to has received financial donations from your organization. When they hear something negative, this group wants to hear your side of the story, but they will tend to give you the benefit of the doubt.

Straddlers

By far the largest group is in the middle of the bell curve. They are not sure whether they should be for you or against you. They have not had much contact with your organization or even paid much attention to the fact that you were in the community. (The truth is, most people are too busy taking care of their own concerns to pay a lot of attention to what goes on around them if it does not directly impact them.)

So these folks will form their opinion about your organization based on information they receive from you and your critics during the crisis. They could go either way, depending on how persuasive and convincing your story is and how well you present it—all subjects for later chapters.

Skeptics

To the right of the straddlers are those folks who are prepared, for some reason, to believe bad things about your organization. This, too, could be for any number of reasons. Some organizations are part of an industry that people view negatively, whether for valid reason or not. (My friends in the chemical industry know that, for years, when public attitude surveys were taken of their impressions of various industries, the chemical industry ranked only slightly higher than tobacco companies and the nuclear industry. They are at a distinct disadvantage when it comes to trying to convince people that they can be trusted.)

Skeptics will therefore give more credence to what is said by the other side rather than believe what your organization says during a crisis.

Splenetics

Okay, so Webster does not have this word in his dictionary! I made it up. All the other words began with an "S" and I wanted a word to fit my model, so just hang in there with me for a moment. I discovered that, in ancient times, people used to believe the spleen was the bodily organ that was the seat of ill temper. An especially irritable and peevish person was thought to have an over-productive spleen. These people are often mad about everything, or they might be okay on every subject except when it comes to your industry or your specific organization. They may hate you for some specific reason. Possibly you fired them or one of their relatives, you dropped them as a vendor, or you had to refuse an unreasonable request they made of you.

If you give these folks an excuse, by having an accident or making a mistake that affects the public, you will surely become the target of splenetic rantings. There is usually nothing you can say that will change their minds and move them to the left on the bell curve.

Target the Middle of the Curve

With all of these audiences in mind, set about addressing your remarks to the three groups in the center. Do not be content just because you can convince your supporters. If your crisis management team goes to the public with a statement that satisfied all of them as they sat around the board room conference table, you may still not communicate properly. Spend time walking in the shoes of the folks in the middle who desperately want to hear an explanation that addresses their needs and concerns.

These middle groups need to have sufficient, solid, believable information. Your organization may want to take a low profile. Someone says, "I know what was said about us was not true, but if we respond, we'll just be keeping the issue alive." While there is a certain amount of truth to this (See Chapter 26 "Considering Your Options if Misquoted or Maligned"), by refusing to respond, you may be depriving the people in the middle of the bell curve of ammunition with which to fight off the assault of your critics. They will have no recourse but to believe what your critics say is true.

On the other hand, do not concern yourself too much with trying to convince the splenetics. It is really like batting your head against a brick wall. You will just exhaust yourself. Surely you should not do anything to further enrage these folks if you can help it. However, do not judge your success by whether or not any of them convert to your point of view.

If you concentrate your efforts on the 80 percent of the people in the middle of this bell curve, and do a good job of communicating with them, you will have done your best and gone a long way toward achieving your objectives.

Figure 5

THE PUBLIC'S CORE VALUES

Health and safety of selves and families

Value of possessions and property

Environmental protection

"Quality of life" issues

Pride in community

Absence of conflict

Freedom from fear

Economic Security

Peer Pressure

Source: "Influencing Public Attitudes: Strategies that Reduce the Media's Power" by James E. Lukaszewski, The Lukaszewski Group Copyright ©1992
Issue Action Publications, p. 11
Used with permission.

11

Addressing the Public's Core Values

As you face your audience, whether they are sitting in front of you at a municipal board meeting or are in their living rooms watching TV or anywhere reading their newspaper, you must recognize what is important to them. Only then can you provide them with the answers they need to hear.

My friend and expert crisis management consultant Jim Lukaszewski has written extensively about this subject, which he calls "The Public's Core Values." He has graciously agreed to let me share his concepts with you. The list shown in Figure 5 was developed after interviews in which people were asked to rate what matters most to them.

Health and Safety of Selves and Families

The health and safety of the individual and his family is ranked first. If anything you have done or could do would hurt a family's health or safety, you will have a serious battle on your hands. This is not hard to understand. Put yourself in the shoes of your facility's neighbors, and I'll wager you would answer the same way.

Value of Possessions and Property

Pocketbook issues rank high. Would an expansion of your

facility reduce your neighbor's property value? Would the recent publicity about accidents, escaped convicts, or wandering mental patients make it harder for this person to sell his house?

Environmental Protection

Approximately 80% of Americans consider themselves "environmentalists." By that they do not mean that they are actively involved in radical organizations that picket facilities or try to shut them down. What they mean is that they care about trying to preserve this planet's air, water and land so that their children and grandchildren have a decent place to live. It would be helpful if, when you speak, you tell your audience that these things are important to you as well. Give them some specific examples of what you are doing in support of the environment.

"Quality of Life"

This is sometimes hard to define, but by looking at some subgroups of this topic, you will understand it better.

Pride in Community: If you do not pay attention to how your company looks aesthetically, your neighbors could be upset with you. Good neighbors don't let their grass grow too long or let weeds take over the flowerbeds or paint chip off the walls.

Absence of Conflict: Most people do not enjoy fighting against such things as the release of smelly fumes, frequent clouds of dust or the rumble of truck traffic through residential neighborhoods.

Freedom from Fear: None of your neighbors wants to have to worry about being awakened in the middle of the night because of an explosion and/or fire at your facility or the escape of a convicted felon or mental patient. This leads right back up to Number 1 on the list. This time, however, it is just the nagging thought that this might happen that hurts their "quality of life."

Economic Security

This is different than the second one, but these issues affect their pocketbooks too. It includes such matters as how your company impacts their ability to make a living. Do you employ them or someone they care about? Do they sell your company products or services? Are the organizations they belong to receiving contributions from you? If the answers to these questions are "yes" and something is happening that threatens those arrangements, they will be concerned.

Note, however, how much less important these items are when compared with the health and safety of themselves and their families. I mention this because I always cringe when I see a company representative answer community questions about health/safety/ environmental concerns by stating how many people the company employs or how much money the company pays in taxes. That is not what concerns your neighbors after an incident has frightened them! In fact, right then many would gladly pay more in taxes to get you out of their town. You cannot buy people's favor. You must earn their trust.

Peer pressure

Last on the list is the fact that people want to be well thought of by their friends and neighbors. This can work for or against you. For example, one of your neighbors is upset about something related to your organization—upset enough to write a petition and take it door-to-door demanding that you be shut down. If one of the higher-ranking items is working in your favor, e.g., you employ a relative of his or his child, this individual is not likely to sign. Even if he just appreciates the way you always plant beautiful flowers at your facility to make the town look nice, or your company supports the annual anti-litter clean-up day that is his pet project, he may be willing to stand up to the peer pressure.

Being aware of the importance people attach to these various core values will make your efforts more effective. Learn as much as you can about where the local people place their values so you do not unknowingly make matters worse. Your best approach is to clearly communicate how much emphasis you place on health, safety, environmental protection, and the economic well-being of the community. Just make sure that your words are backed up by your past record and your current actions!

12

A Mid-Course Summary

U p to this point, we've been reviewing what you should have in place before a crisis erupts. To summarize:

- You should have a Crisis Communications Plan established that covers all the various things that could go wrong. It should list who will be mobilized or contacted for each type of crisis and how you can get hold of them day or night.

- You should have selected a spokesperson who embodies as many of the characteristics listed in Chapter 5 as possible, and you should have identified a secondary spokesperson as backup.

- You should have identified who would be mobilized as the Crisis Management Team for various types of crises. Hopefully, you have told them they would be on the team and you have encouraged them to give serious thought to what they would recommend doing and saying if the particular scenarios occur. Better still, ask them to bring their draft plan to a staff meeting where it can be debated and refined.

  (HINT: To ensure that this kind of pre-planning occurs, call a special surprise staff meeting for the express purpose of working through your response to an imaginary crisis. This kind of role-playing, which we do for a half-day in my crisis management media training workshops, is always instructive.)

- You should have considered who your audiences would be for the various kinds of crises. You should have enhanced your internal communications and set up outreach efforts to establish good community relations before a crisis hits. Things like media backgrounders, speeches to local groups, and an Open Door policy will convince many people to give you the benefit of the doubt during a crisis. If your own employees are unhappy with you and your outside audiences have not heard from you or about you, you will have a much harder job during a crisis.

If all of these "should's" are in place, the next step is to make sure those you've chosen to speak with the press are well trained to do so.

At a minimum, four people in your organization (the highest-ranking official, the spokesperson and their back-ups) should have undergone professional media training. The techniques of dealing with the media usually do not come naturally, even to the most competent leaders. It is a whole different skill set from what makes a person effective as a plant manager, executive director, municipal official or CEO. This media training should include hands-on practice with some realistic role-playing to help reinforce the theoretical instruction.

Working with the Press

Before you actually go out to meet the reporter, make sure to review some general concepts of communicating with the media during a crisis. You need to have a positive frame of mind. There are some things you should strive for and some things you should try hard to avoid.

Figure 6

THE 10 "C's" OF GOOD CRISIS COMMUNICATIONS

1. Be COOPERATIVE	6. Be CONSISTENT
2. Provide CONTROL	7. Be CLEAR
3. Demonstrate CARING And CONCERN	8. Be CONCISE
4. Demonstrate COMPETENCE	9. Keep CURRENT
5. Be CREDIBLE	10. Act With CALM

13

The 10 "C's" of Good Crisis Communications

Hopefully, you have done all of the preparation recommended in the previous chapters. Now comes the moment of truth. Members of the media have arrived, either in person or on the telephone. They know something has happened and are anxious to learn more. If your spokesperson exhibits the ten characteristics described in this chapter and shown in Figure 6, your organization stands a good chance of getting fair and objective coverage from the press.

1. Be Cooperative

It is imperative that, from the very start, you establish an atmosphere of cooperation. The media has its job to do. Reporters need to let the public know what is going on. In cases involving public safety, this need is urgent, and they will have no patience if you don't respond to them immediately. Where public safety is not involved but your organization's reputation is at stake, any hint that you are not going to cooperate with them will do two things:

(1) It will give them a negative impression of your organization, which will be reflected in the news coverage; and

(2) It will inevitably lead the reporters to the conclusion that

Figure 7

Date	Time	Person Calling/Affiliation (news organization, official, etc.)	Phone # of Caller	Calling for	Subject (Be Specific)	Call Taken By

EMERGENCY CALL LOG

you have something to hide. Their journalistic instincts will cause them to dig deeper. Someone once compared the media to a junkyard dog saying, "If you don't voluntarily feed the media, they will root around in your garbage until they find something."

By asking for a comment from your organization, the media is giving you an opportunity to tell your side of the story. If you brush them off with a "no comment," you cannot later complain that they didn't get it right. If you leave an information vacuum, someone else will fill it, and you can be assured your critics will not tell the story the way you would like. Remember, as once stated in Dun's Business Month, "If a company does not manage its own news event, someone else is sure to MISmanage it."

2. Provide Control

When the media arrives at the site of an incident, they should be directed to a specific area that was previously designated in the organization's Crisis Communications Plan. The media should be told that if they want the most current information, they should stay in the Media Center and that someone will be with them soon.

This Media Center should not be close to the Incident Command Post (in the case of an operational incident) or the conference room where the Crisis Management Team (CMT) is meeting. You do not want the media conducting impromptu interviews with members of the CMT who are on their way to the bathroom! But the rooms should be close enough that the spokesperson can, without too much trouble, shuttle back and forth, keeping the media supplied with frequent updates.

If the interviews are being conducted on the telephone, the spokesperson should keep an accurate telephone log. On this one sheet of paper, as shown in Figure 7 on the previous page, record who you talked to and what was said. By referring back to this, a spokesperson can see who has received what news and update each reporter so they all get the same information. (Providing one media source with more information than you give the others is a dangerous game that usually backfires. You make one person happy and everyone else mad.)

3. Demonstrate <u>Caring and Concern</u>

It is absolutely critical for the spokesperson to convey early on that the organization is sincerely concerned about those who might perceive themselves as victims of the situation. This is particularly important if people have been injured or if the environment has been damaged or threatened. The public will not regard kindly an organization that does not demonstrate that it cares about people or the environment. Any perceived callousness will create a negative impression that can last for a long time.

Some people may remember the horror story of several dozen employees who died when a flash fire raced through a chicken nugget manufacturing facility in North Carolina many years ago. Management had locked the emergency exits to prevent employees from pilfering food and/or taking unauthorized smoke breaks. People piled up at the emergency exits and died. This tragedy was made even worse because it was *three days* before a representative of the company offered any word of condolence to the families of those who died.

I can only imagine that the organization's lawyers advised them not to say or do anything that could work against them in a lawsuit. However, there is simply no excuse for an organization not showing sympathy and concern, offering to do whatever they can for survivors or relatives following a tragedy. Besides being the right and humane thing to do, judges and juries in the inevitable lawsuits will look to further punish any organization which appears cold and heartless. Expressions of sympathy and concern are always in order, although they must be done carefully to avoid unnecessary admissions of liability.

Lawyers may be uncomfortable with this approach. Public relations and communications professionals are equally uncomfortable with anything less. This is when the CEO has to shoulder the responsibility, listen to both sides, and decide what is in the best interests of the organization. Usually, with some hard work, a balance can be found that will satisfy both.

4. Demonstrate <u>Competence</u>

When the spokesperson begins that first interview, she must be prepared. The basics of the 5 W's and an H (who, what, when, where, why, and how) should be arranged in a statement which, as clearly as possible, lays out the facts as they are known at that time. Perhaps all of the answers (particularly the why and how) may not be known in the early stages of a crisis. But by presenting what IS known in a logical way, the organization gives the appearance of being on top of the situation. This will make reporters more comfortable in using them as the primary source for updates. If the spokesperson approaches the reporters thinking she can just "wing it," she is inviting disaster. Rapid-fire questions will quickly lead to a lot of stumbling around, conflicting statements, indications of nervousness, and a general impression of incompetence.

5. Be <u>Credible</u>

Your credibility is an organization's most important asset during tough times. In most cases, credibility—or the lack thereof—is based on past experiences. If your organization has been straightforward and honest with the press and the public in the past, even when the news has not been good, the media will give you the benefit of the doubt. If, on the other hand, you have either lied to them or withheld important information, they will be predisposed not to trust what you are telling them now. As you proceed with the current incident, you must guard your credibility, not only for the crisis at hand, but for all future dealings with the media.

NEVER LIE. Once you start, even with a small "white" lie, these things have a way of snowballing out of control. Your lie will almost surely be found out, and the short-term pain you have temporarily avoided will not be worth the long-term damage to your reputation.

Protection of your credibility also means that you must always be *sure* of the information you provide. NEVER SPECULATE! As Pentagon spokesman Captain Steve Pietropaoli said when questioned about the NATO bombings in Serbia, "The only thing worse than making you wait for the facts is giving you facts that turn out not to be facts."

If you are not sure of the answer to a question, say so. An honest, "I cannot verify that information as of yet; when I can, I will get back to you," is vastly preferable to giving the media a good guess. You will often have to retract such speculation and then your credibility is brought into question. Former U.S. Attorney General Janet Reno had it right when she refused to speculate on the outcome of a trial, saying, "I always wait until a jury has spoken before I anticipate what they will do."

Rest assured that you will be pressed to speculate. The media and the public want to know why something has happened. Your investigation may take days or weeks. You will grow tired of being asked about it. A dramatic example of this was the crash of TWA Flight 800 off of Long Island, New York some years ago. It took months of hard work to drag up the pieces of the airplane from the bottom of the ocean and put them together to try to understand why that plane went down. In an atmosphere where the possibility of a terrorist bomb was uppermost in the minds of many people, authorities were continuously pressed—within two to three days of the accident—to explain what had caused the tragedy. When the answer could not be given quickly, countless rumors and theories were circulated, including everything from a terrorist bomb to an errant government missile.

All you can do is continue to provide what you know to be a fact. Say, "The incident is still under investigation" while you work on determining the facts. A good way to approach refusing to speculate is to say something like this: "It is our company's position never to speculate at times like this, so I cannot tell you that, but

- what I can tell you is...."
- I can tell you about the process that is underway to get the facts."
- as soon as I have verifiable information, I will get back to you."

6. Be <u>Consistent</u>

This characteristic is also linked to credibility. If you provide information based only on verified facts, then you will remain consistent. The need for consistency also underscores the advisability of designating a single spokesperson who is aware of what has been said to whom. If the situation requires more than one spokesperson, then someone needs to play the role of "gatekeeper" who coordinates what various people are communicating. For example, if the incident is serious enough to warrant the involvement of the highest-ranking official of the organization, the initial spokesperson must thoroughly brief the CEO on all that has been communicated so far. If the incident is technical in nature and requires that others in the organization speak about their areas of expertise, they must be cognizant of what has previously been said. When different people start telling the organization's story without this kind of coordination, slightly differing versions may give the impression that someone is not telling the truth.

7. Be <u>Clear</u>

Of course, a spokesperson must speak distinctly and not mumble. But, more importantly, she must speak in a language that laypeople understand. Each industry has special terms, concepts and abbreviations. Those in that industry are so familiar with them, they become second nature. It is easy to let this jargon slip into your public statements. If it does, the vast majority of the public will not have a CLUE what you are talking about. The result? The public will be confused or angry. They may think that you are trying to use some "mumbo-jumbo" to pull the wool over their eyes.

One way to avoid this is to take your prepared statement (or the major points you plan to make during a session with the media) and read it out loud to someone outside of your organization, or at least to someone not as familiar with the issue at hand. Spouses and adolescent children come in handy here, especially when you remember that even the *Wall Street Journal* seeks to write at an eighth grade reading level to insure comprehension.

Ask these folks if they understand the points you are trying to make. Have them indicate any areas that are unclear, either because you use jargon or because the explanation was too complex for them to follow. Rework the material until it is as easy as possible for non-technical people to grasp.

If you are in a more extemporaneous situation—like a give-and-take with a reporter—you do not have the advantage of a printed script. Then you must be extra alert, catching yourself when you slip into jargon. If it is a face-to-face interview, you must be conscious of the body language of the reporter. Is he frowning and looking totally confused? Do you see the MEGO (My Eyes Glaze Over) phenomenon?

If you are working with a colleague, he should watch for these signs while you are speaking. Then he could step in to explain the special term or clarify a technical point with an explanation that relates to the everyday world.

Reporters cannot be expected to understand the fine points of every organization's business or their terminology. They are usually generalists. If you use obscure terminology, the reporter could make an educated guess in order not to appear stupid. That guess may be wrong, thereby resulting in an unintentional and avoidable negative slant on the story. You might read the story the next day and claim indignantly, "That's NOT what I said!" But when you think back on it, you may find that you slipped into using some technical terms that left your points open to misinterpretation.

Of course, you must be careful not to talk down to people too. What is needed is a clear explanation that doesn't use technical language, not simply a slow and loud sentence that will insult someone's intelligence.

One more word of caution: a major impediment to clear communication is the very human tendency to attempt to impress our audience and reporters with our knowledge. Just because we know a big word for something does not mean we need to use it! If a simpler word is more easily understood, use it instead. A crisis is NOT the time to try to impress people with how expansive your vocabulary is.

As an illustration, see how much of the following paragraph you understand.

A geriatric human female proceeded to a storage compartment for the purpose of procuring a fragment of osseous tissue from an unidentified deceased specimen to transfer to an indigent carnivorous domesticated mammal, *canis familiaris*, family *canidae*. Upon arrival at her destination, she found the storage compartment in denuded condition, with the consequence that the indigent carnivore was deprived of the intended donation.

Did you figure it out? Did you have to go all the way to the end before you recognized the children's nursery rhyme "Old Mother Hubbard?" In amongst the big words, the message was totally lost. But don't we sometimes find ourselves—especially when composing press statements—writing like this? We think we have to be formal.

Some people apparently believe that the use of technical terms will impress people. In reality, it often prevents you from achieving your most important goal—clearly explaining a situation and communicating your message.

8. Be <u>Concise</u>

Brevity is an art. When dealing with the media, it is especially important. If you say more than you need to, one of two things will happen:

(1) You open up a whole new line of questioning that you wish had not been broached.

(2) You invite the editors of the radio/TV show or the newspaper to edit your remarks. If you cannot communicate your major points briefly enough to fit their space, they will select what they want. You may not be at all pleased with the result. If you talk about unnecessary details or ramble too much, they may simply edit out your comments completely.

The need for conciseness is especially critical with the electronic media. In a small town, something that has happened at your organization may warrant a big story on the local cable network. But a "big" story here is still only three minutes long. Of that, you may be allotted 30 seconds to provide your statement, explanation, or comments. If you are located in a larger city or metropolitan area, each story usually lasts on average 40-50 seconds. Then you have only 7-10 seconds to make your point! That isn't much time, but if you practice, you can do it.

In the print media, you should follow the "inverted pyramid" style of writing. Put the most important statements in the first sentence or two of the press release. (Usually these are the 5 W's and an H and your expression of caring and concern.) Then proceed with supporting details in a prioritized way. Then, if an editor has to cut the statement to fit the printed page, he'll start cutting from the bottom and the most important points will still be communicated.

9. Remain <u>Current</u>

In a long, drawn-out incident that spans many hours or days, you must update the media at regular intervals. If you do not, they will begin to search around for others who will provide more current information. The comments of these other people, especially if they are upset about what has happened, could cast your organization in a very negative light.

Make sure you clearly state when and where you will provide statements and updates. Stick to your schedule and be dependable.

10. Act <u>Calm</u>

In a crisis, it is sometimes very difficult to be calm. Adrenaline is pumping and nerves are on edge. However, it is vital that your spokesperson *acts* calm. She can't appear on camera in an agitated, wild-eyed state. That will not help solve the problem. In fact, it will exacerbate it.

NEVER LOSE YOUR TEMPER. Conflict is news. The media loves it. Witness this example of then President George H.W. Bush when he was campaigning against Bill Clinton. He was giving a speech one day when he was interrupted by a woman in the audience who demanded to know what his administration was doing about the situation of servicemen who had been designated as Missing in Action (MIA) during the Vietnam War. Five times he calmly dealt with her interruptions. But the sixth time, totally frustrated, he yelled, "SHUT UP!"

Does anyone have any doubt about what appeared on every channel's evening news program? Was this reporting fair? No. But was it news? Yes. Only a few people heard the full story of how politely he dealt with her the previous five times. The unfortunate thing is that the impression left with the vast majority of TV viewers that night was of a cold and uncaring President who could not deal compassionately with this poor woman whose husband had been designated as an MIA for so many years. The public sympathized with her. Because the President could not control his temper in these admittedly trying circumstances, he came off looking very bad indeed.

If you are ever tempted to lose your temper in public, no matter how justified you feel it might be, remember that your outburst is likely to become a media moment. It is NOT the way you want to be remembered.

Try to keep these "10 C's" in mind when you step in front of the TV cameras or hold your interviews with print reporters. For specific examples of how this looks in the midst of a crisis, look at the chapter in Section VIII that shows how New York City Mayor Rudy Giuliani implemented each one in the aftermath of the terrorist attacks on the World Trade Center.

CHAPTER
14

Two "C's" to Avoid

N ow that you've reviewed the "10 C's" you want to strive to achieve, here is a quick reminder of two "C's" you should avoid when the situation is serious and tensions are running high.

Figure 8

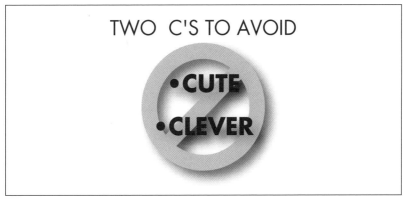

TWO C'S TO AVOID

• CUTE

• CLEVER

If you have been invited to speak before the local service club or a church organization in your town to explain what your organization is all about, you might want to be entertaining. You might even use some well thought-out humor. In that situation, you want people to see you as a "nice guy."

However, when someone has been hurt, there's been a threat to the environment, or a member of your organization has been accused of serious wrongdoing, it is totally inappropriate to treat it lightly. People will resent your flippant attitude.

There is a special warning here for those times when you are in front of the TV cameras. As you head toward the room where you will meet with the press or address the gathered public, be very conscious of your demeanor. You do not want to appear as if you are on your last walk on death row. But neither do you want to appear cocky and unconcerned about the situation. Your colleagues may think they are doing you a favor by trying to break the tension with a humorous remark. If you laugh or even smirk a little, this could be caught on camera. How embarrassing to you and your whole organization to see this footage played as the anchor is introducing the story, leaving the unmistakable impression that the organization does not care about what has happened.

CHAPTER

15

"No Comment" is a No-No

If you really want the media to dig deeply into a story, here's a tip: Say "NO COMMENT!" and walk swiftly away from the TV camera or the reporter, or slam down the phone. That should do it. Those two words translate in almost every reporter's mind to "Guilty as charged." They immediately wonder "What are they afraid of? There must be a big story here!"

I have encouraged you in previous chapters to cooperate with the media when they come calling. Wouldn't you rather tell your story than have someone else do it for you? You stand a much better chance of getting objective coverage if you provide your views on the issue. With the proper training, you can make your case convincingly and end up enhancing your organization's public image.

Must You Always Comment?

No. There certainly are legitimate situations where your best response to a reporter's question might be that you cannot answer them, at least not right then. But you still should not use the two specific words "No comment." It sounds rude. It looks bad in print. There is no reason to be so curt with reporters, especially if you want them to act responsibly toward you.

Some Legitimate Reasons to Decline Comment

There are times when you may not be able to or want to answer a particular question. If that is the case, you are much better off to politely explain why you cannot answer it. Here is some suggested wording you can use if the situation truly warrants it:

"This matter is under litigation and we are not permitted to comment at this time as it might prejudice the case."

"I am not qualified to answer that question as it is outside my area of expertise. You should pose that question to _____."

"To answer that question risks revealing proprietary information which could negatively impact our competitive position in the marketplace."

"It would be inappropriate for me to reveal the names of the dead (or injured) until we are sure their relatives have been notified."

"You are asking me to make a judgment for another person which is not appropriate; I would prefer that you ask him."

"It would not be useful to speculate on this hypothetical situation."

(For publicly owned companies): "The Securities and Exchange Commission prohibits the release of this kind of information when such release could give rise to unfair trading practices."

"You are asking for my personal opinion, which is not appropriate in this situation."

"We have not yet seen a copy of the document to which you refer; therefore we are not prepared to make a comment at this time."

"I simply do not know the answer to your question. I will attempt to find an answer and get back to you by _____."
(Try to determine their deadline.)

Most reporters will recognize the validity of these reasonable responses and move on. If they sense "stonewalling," you have just added fuel to the fire.

In Chapter 19, I will discuss the valuable media training technique of "bridging" from the question asked to one of the major messages you want to communicate. Here I will just point out that you can sometimes move from a question to which you might be tempted to blurt out "No comment!" to something which the reporters will find is quotable and you will be seen as cooperative. For example: "I cannot tell you that, but what I *can* do is explain the process we will be undertaking to get those facts." Or you could sidestep a reporter's attempt to get you to speculate by saying, "One of the things we pride ourselves on here is that we do not assume any information which may later be proven to be inaccurate. Our goal is to complete our investigation and have facts for you by Wednesday."

But Don't be a "Baghdad Bob"

While all this said above is true, the war in Iraq in 2003 did provide the world with a classic example of how sometimes it is best to just keep quiet. The allied forces were only a few miles outside of Baghdad and the sounds of bombs and gunfire were audible in the city. Meanwhile the Iraqi Information Minister made statements to the city's residents reassuring them that they were safe and that reports of advancing troops were just rumors meant to frighten them. He only looked foolish and instantly became the butt of comedians' jokes. In this case, silence would have been preferable.

Under normal circumstances, however, just saying "No comment!" is like waving a red flag in front of a bull. Run for your life and prepare for a full-blown crisis!

It sometimes takes courage to be proactive,

but it can be the best move to make.

16

Going "Above and Beyond"

You have probably heard the military phrase that someone went "above and beyond the call of duty." This is also an important concept in media relations.

Let us assume that you are prepared to cooperate with the media if—or I should say *when*—they come to call. You will give them the information that they need to write their story. But I'd like you to consider doing even more.

Let's say you become aware of a situation that is building in your organization or your industry. You think that it is likely to come to the attention of the media at some point. Why not proactively broach the subject? If you do, you can achieve three important things:

(1) The media immediately gets the sense that this issue cannot be all that bad.

(2) It takes all the joy out of a reporter's desire to engage in investigative muckraking.

(3) It provides you with the opportunity to be the one who shapes the story.

How It Works

Let me give you an example. In 1978, the chemical industry had to comply with legislation known as the Superfund Amendment and Re-authorization Act (SARA), which required companies to report their emissions of certain chemicals to the air, water, and land. The catchy name for this data was the Toxic Release Inventory or TRI.

I vividly remember the discussion that occurred within the industry. There was a great deal of fear and trepidation about how the media was going to report on this data once it was released on July 1st. Surely, it was said, when reporters saw what appeared to be large volumes of pollutants being discharged, there would be sensationalistic headlines and extremely negative stories.

The only publication requirement at that time was that the data had to be submitted to the Local Emergency Planning Committee (LEPC), a governmental body at the county level. Back then, most LEPC's were like ours—not well organized. As part of an unfunded mandate, it had neither sufficient staff nor money to be effective. We recognized that the LEPC would be hard pressed to properly organize all of the TRI data they would be receiving. We surmised that, if a concerned citizen requested TRI information from the LEPC, it would take them a while to fulfill the request. Some managers cautioned, "Wait and see if anybody asks for it. Why go borrowing trouble?"

As Manager of Public Affairs, external communications were my responsibility. I was confident that the public *would* want to know about our TRI data. Before I went to work at the chemical company, I had been a member of the local chapter of the League of Women Voters (LWV). Environmental protection was one of the planks in their platform. I knew that, as soon as it became known that this data had to be filed, one of my LWV colleagues would be asking for it. I also knew that undue delays in obtaining that information would lead to frustration and anger. I imagined negative stories in the LWV monthly bulletin and the local newspapers as well.

To avoid the appearance that the company was attempting to hide this data, I suggested that we publish the information and place it openly in local municipal halls and libraries. I still remember the shocked looks on the faces of several members of the management team when I brought up the subject. To their credit, however, they were willing to discuss it—especially once the company president said the idea was worthy of further consideration.

What eventually developed was a 40-page notebook. The TRI data was included, of course. However, we were able to present it in a way that we thought would be more palatable—breaking down annual air emission figures to pounds per hour, for instance. We also made sure there was a clear statement that these were estimated figures and an explanation of why we were confident that the estimates vastly overstated the actual case. We also used the opportunity to provide local citizens with accurate scientific definitions of some of the scary sounding words like "hazardous," "toxic," and "carcinogen," which they would probably be hearing or reading when the media began reporting on the TRI data after July 1st.

Surrounding the actual TRI data were chapters about the company's history, products, processes, safety and environmental programs, emergency response capabilities, and the benefits brought to the community by our being part of it.

This binder was quite an undertaking for our small company. It took time to pull it all together, but it was ready by the end of the day on June 29th. Our plan was to deliver it to the town halls, libraries, and local newspaper offices. (Yes, we had actually agreed to that! If it were public information, why not make the reporter's job easier instead of making him have to work so hard?)

On June 30th, just as I was leaving my office to deliver the binders, my phone rang. "Hi! This is Ruth from the newspaper. I know you guys have to report by tomorrow on all of your emissions. I was wondering if you could give me a 'heads up' on this?"

I replied immediately. "I'm glad you called, Ruth. I have in my hand your copy of the binder we have put together that explains what this TRI data is all about and provides our data. Will you be in your office for the next half-hour? I can be right over."

You could have heard a pin drop. She obviously was not expecting that answer. She was sure she'd have to dig for the information. I thought I could hear the hissing sound of the wind coming out of her investigative sails. "Sure," she said, "come on over."

Of course our whole management team held our collective breath until the newspaper hit our front stoops the next day. What a loud sigh of relief could be heard as we read the headline, "Company Makes Emissions Data Available to the Public." The whole story was about the fact that we were being so open about it. The article didn't even mention the tons per year of our various chemicals going into the atmosphere. A subsequent story included a list of the "Dirty Dozen" of the county (those whose emission figures were among the twelve highest), but our name was not listed. Even had we appeared there, I am convinced that we would have gotten better treatment because we had gone "above and beyond" what was absolutely required.

Another Example

In another instance, when the company received a bomb threat, I suggested to management that we be the ones to call the local media. At first they thought I had really lost my mind, but they were eventually persuaded that this was the right course of action. By my contacting the local media, I could effectively plead for them to use discretion in the reporting so as not to stimulate a rash of copycat incidents.

The media cooperated beautifully. Some didn't even mention it. Others wrote a brief, factual account that showed that the company responded appropriately to protect its employees and the community. Had they heard the call go out over the emergency scanner for the bomb-sniffing dogs to be sent to the plant, a reporter and photographer would have been immediately dispatched. This would have made a much bigger story, possibly encouraging others to try to cause the same level of excitement.

While volunteering information to the media may be a strange idea to some, it is something you should at least consider. It can benefit your company image and your credibility with the media tremendously.

A message you don't want to get from your office staff:

"It's a Mr. Mike Wallace on Line 1."

17

Strive for "One-Day, Local-Only" Coverage

One of my favorite sayings is, "Bad news is like dead fish. It doesn't get better with time."

If something bad has happened to your organization, management often finds the incident embarrassing and would rather keep quiet about it. One or more of your employees may have exercised poor judgment. Your equipment may have broken down. A system didn't operate the way it should have. Procedures weren't followed properly.

When this becomes public knowledge, the media will have some hard questions for you.

Pain Avoidance is Tempting...

When those questions come, many people are tempted to fall into the patterns learned in early childhood. I am assuming here that lying is simply not an option. Remember from Chapter 13 the need to maintain your credibility. When you step before a TV camera or microphone, you NEVER want to jeopardize that credibility.

What I have seen adults do, however, is word their answers so they can delay as long as possible admitting that their organization did something wrong—or at least did not do everything they should have. They hem and haw and try to drag things out, hoping the media will lose interest. This is an old trick children use to avoid painful consequences.

... But It Isn't Worth It

Mature adults should realize that, once it is clear what caused an incident, it is better to step up to the plate and provide accurate information as soon as possible, whether it is embarrassing or not. The public wants, and sometimes needs, to know *why* something has happened. They will usually speculate—sometimes wildly—until they get an answer. The press will keep digging until they are satisfied.

Isn't it worse to pull the adhesive bandage off a hairy arm s-l-o-w-l-y than it is to give it one good rip and have done with it? The end result is the same.

There is a very good reason to admit the embarrassing news. The situation won't get better with time. If you can provide the local media with the basics (the 5 W's and an H again!), they can write the story that day and then forget about it. If you delay providing any part of the basics, you are practically guaranteeing a follow-up story. Repetition the next day makes the story assume added importance and puts your organization's name in a negative light one more time.

Worse still, if a story appears in a local publication or on a local TV news show for several days in a row, you increase your chances of becoming news to a media channel with a larger audience. When the metropolitan area news organizations start calling, you will rue the day you didn't just tell the media the whole story.

What to Do When You Cannot Provide All the Information

Of course there will be times when you cannot confidently

supply all of the information on the first day. You may know the basics of what happened—when, where, and to whom an incident occurred—but you have not yet fully uncovered why it happened. Sometimes painstaking investigations are required.

Being anxious to supply as much information as you can in order to achieve one-day, local-only coverage does NOT mean you should violate the rule against speculation. In statements to the media, you should confine yourself to facts that you are quite sure are true. Before the investigation into the cause of a fire at a manufacturing facility is complete, you may have learned that employees saw a pile of oily rags near the furnace just prior to their seeing the furnace explode in a ball of flame. In such an instance, you could say with reasonable assurance: "What appears to have happened is..." Some people call these "weasel-words," but on occasions like this they may be appropriate. If the cause of the fire is truly unknown, the traditional "The cause of the fire is still under investigation" will have to suffice until more facts are confirmed.

The objective is to be as forthcoming as you can be. When you finally do know the cause, you should let the media know. Don't let them "dig it up" on their own. They will decide at that time if it is worth another story, or if it has become old news.

Admitting Mistakes Is Usually the Best Approach

In most cases, when something has gone wrong, something could have been done to prevent it. Somewhere, somehow, someone made a mistake or a grave error in judgment. Your legal advisors may cringe at the thought of publicly admitting this. But if someone feels like a victim, he will probably be considering a lawsuit anyway. You are trying to minimize the damage to your corporate reputation.

It has been proven time and time again that the public can forgive an organization if it honestly admits it made a mistake. How many of you remember the odometer scandal associated with Chrysler Corporation? If you don't, or if the details are fuzzy, it is most likely because it was handled right. In fact, it has become a classic in the annals of public relations books. Here are the details.

In 1987, Chrysler Corporation and two of its executives were criminally indicted for taking new cars off the assembly line, driving them as much as 400 miles with the odometers disconnected, and then selling them as new vehicles.

Initially, the legal stance of the corporation was that they had done nothing wrong. Negative public opinion began to mount. Lee Iacocca, Chairman of Chrysler and a man known for years for his tendency for straight talk, held a news conference. In it he called these actions "dumb." While stating that he had personally not been aware of the practices until a few months before the indictment was made, he nevertheless took responsibility. His lawyers must have choked.

Iacocca went further. It had been discovered that 40 cars had been sold as new when they had actually been involved in serious accidents and repaired. Iacocca termed this "unforgivable." Not only did he admit wrongdoing and take responsibility in both of these instances; he went on to make amends. The 40 people who bought the damaged cars were given new vehicles. Those who had purchased automobiles whose odometers had been disconnected were given expanded warranties.

The company was fined $300,000. But Iacocca had realized that he was facing the loss of faith of the public in their products, and this was something he was determined to avoid.

His judgment was proven correct. In a survey conducted some months later, 67% of the people surveyed said they felt the corporation's response had been adequate. Even more telling, their stock price remained stable and there was no drop in sales. Many editorials were written which praised Iacocca for his honesty, his willingness to step up to the plate to take responsibility, and the efforts to make amends.

What the public cannot forgive is when individuals and organizations lie, cover up, or stonewall the press. Those actions simply spur reporters to dig deeper, and the public will relish hearing what they unearth.

What is usually required is a simple but sincere apology. "We are sorry that this happened. We made a mistake. Here is what we plan to do to make amends, and we pledge to do whatever we can to minimize the chances that it will happen again." Painful, perhaps, but certainly preferable to the alternatives.

Standing in stark contrast, of course, is the Firestone tire debacle mentioned previously. Years before the crisis broke wide open in 2000, the manufacturer knew there were serious problems with their tires in Latin America. The Ford Motor Company became embroiled in the crisis and their corporate reputation ended up sullied as well. Both organizations have been named in countless lawsuits.

In hindsight, wouldn't it have been better for Firestone — not to mention the hundreds of innocent victims — if they had admitted their problems and started the recall when they first knew about the problem?

If you've made a mistake, admit it, apologize, accept the punishment and public beating that will surely come, fix the problem, and find out how you can minimize the chance that it will happen again.

When it comes to organizations not being willing to admit problems and ferret out root causes, there is no more disturbing example than the sexual abuse scandal of the Catholic Church. Rumors and sporadic allegations of improper sexual activities between priests and minor boys had been around for decades. It was assumed by many that people were paid to keep silent. But in January of 2002, the horrific scope of the scandal became known. As weeks went by, more and more men came forward to report abuse. Yet still, for months, the church hierarchy attempted to minimize the problem and make excuses. These evasive attempts infuriated more people until there was a veritable flood of victims making their pain public.

It wasn't until April of 2002 that the Pope finally called the U.S. cardinals to Rome. Only then was a strong statement of "zero tolerance" issued. As weeks passed, the interpretation of "zero tolerance" was watered down. Boston Cardinal Bernard F. Law, the man at the epicenter of the controversy, consistently refused to take responsibility and did not resign until forced to do so almost a year after the scandal broke. By then the Catholic Church was talking of bankruptcy and many faithful Catholics had left the organized church.

One can only speculate how many young men would have been spared their physical and emotional pain if the hierarchy of the church had taken the appropriate actions early on. Yes, it would have been embarrassing, but the consequences of covering it all up were devastating for everyone.

SECTION

V

Developing and Presenting
Your Messages

Now you are finally ready to consider what you say and do not say. Spend quality time working with your colleagues to plan this important communication effort. With the spotlight of a crisis shining on you, you do not want to try to "wing it." There are some useful techniques here to help you get your message delivered professionally and remembered by your audience.

If you have done your preparation for an interview thoroughly, there should be no question from a reporter that catches you off guard.

18

Being Prepared for the Most Likely Questions

At the first meeting of their Crisis Management Team (CMT) during a crisis, many organizations attempt to put together a prepared statement in the hope that they will have a chance to read it to the reporters. I'd like to suggest a better method of preparing for the upcoming interviews.

As soon as reporters hear about a newsworthy situation, questions pop into their minds. They will find a way to ask them. It's their job. They may extend you the opportunity to make a statement, and you should develop one. My point here, however, is that the best way to start the process of preparing your response is to go through the exercise of thinking about the questions you will most likely be asked.

Brainstorming the Questions

This is really not a hard thing to do. There are several ways to approach it.

(1) *Put yourselves firmly in the shoes of those most immediately impacted by the situation (facility neighbors, customers, supporters, patients and their families, taxpayers, etc.).*

Forget your advanced degree or your technical knowledge.

Pretend your mother or spouse or child is the one affected and think about what you and they would want to know. The most obvious questions follow the pattern of the 5 W's and an H (which you are probably tired of hearing about by now).

- <u>Who</u> is involved?
- <u>What</u> happened exactly?
- <u>What</u> was the cause?
- <u>What</u> went wrong?
- <u>Where</u> is the impacted area?
- <u>When</u> did it occur? (Is it still ongoing?)
- <u>When</u> will more information be available?
- <u>Why</u> did this happen?
- <u>How</u> did you respond?

But go beyond these basics. While standing in the shoes of these people, think of what else you would like to know. Jot down all of these questions. You can go back and choose the most important ones later.

(2) *Review case studies of previous similar incidents so you can learn what is most often on the minds of people in the midst of crisis.*

Crisis consultant Jim Lukaszewski has compiled a list of the most frequently asked questions based on his more than 20 years of experience. With his permission, I've included some questions from his list. If you practice your answers to these, you will be well on the road to being prepared.

- Couldn't you have prevented this?
- Is it safe for me and my family here?
- How do you know the situation is under control?

- Why didn't you tell us about the possibility of this problem sooner?

- Do you care about what has happened?

- How can we trust you again?

- How will you compensate us for the damage?

You get the idea. Depending on your type of business and the situations you could face, think along these lines for a while and I'm sure you will come up with many other questions.

(3) *Use a focus group.*

This is especially effective, but it does take some time to pull it together. It would be appropriate, for instance, if you were going to be requesting a facility expansion at your current location. When a chemical plant with which I am familiar was required to go through a mandated public process to re-permit their on-site wastewater incinerator, they knew there would be lots of questions from the neighbors.

They cleverly decided to kill two birds with one stone. They felt it was important to inform the employees about the permitting process. They used the opportunity of meeting with them to: (a) educate those employees not familiar with the operations of the incinerator; (b) inform all employees about the permitting process that was ahead of them; and (c) solicit questions, particularly from the non-technical staff, which would probably be similar to those asked by plant neighbors.

Being able to keep all of this internal was extremely valuable and provided the company with significant insights into issues and concerns they had not necessarily considered important.

Develop Your Answers

Once you have made a list of the most likely questions, start composing good answers. It is a very enlightening process, and often somewhat surprising too. What seem like simple questions can be very hard to answer.

"What is this stuff anyway?"

"How dangerous is this situation?"

"How do you KNOW it's safe for me and my family to live next door to your operations?"

You should not expect to be able to pull satisfactory answers together for these "simple questions" off the top of your head.

Probably THE most important question to prepare for is (with apologies to my mother) the "Oh, s___!" question. (It was once again Jim Lukaszewski who taught me this technical term.) This is the question you hope no one asks—the one where you don't have much hard data to support your answer, or the one that could open up a huge bucket of worms if not handled just right. It is not a good idea to just pray that question won't be asked. Assume it *will* be asked, and do the best job you can in preparing your answer. Then you can pray no one will think of it!

Put down on paper your initial draft answers to all of these questions. Read the answers out loud to your colleagues on the CMT. Get them to critique these answers, offering insights from their areas of expertise. Wordsmith them accordingly. Ask for help from your corporate communications experts or outside public relations counsel. As a final test, run the answers by some non-technical office staff to see if they understand them and are convinced or persuaded by your presentation.

Practice Your Answers Until You've "Got" It

Once you have reasonably worded answers—ones that are open to a minimum of misinterpretation—commit the major points to memory. Then practice them until they sound natural and can therefore be delivered with conviction. You can't read these answers from a piece of paper if you hope to be believed.

Preparing for a session of tough questions, whether from reporters or the public, takes the same skills used in athletics or space travel—practice, practice, practice. Repetition makes it become second nature. Then when the moment arrives when people are glued to their TV sets to watch you standing in the glaring lights of a TV camera—you can make your points clearly and with conviction.

Heading off to your interview without two or three major positive points firmly ingrained in your mind is a serious mistake.

19

Creating "Must Air" Messages

As important as it is to think through the questions you are most likely to be asked, you need to go on to the next step. You could do a good job of answering all of the reporter's questions and still not communicate what you want people to know and understand. You cannot depend on the reporter to ask the right questions.

Therefore, before you step in front of a TV camera or a reporter, think about the **three major points** that you want your audience to remember. These overriding messages have been dubbed by some media trainers as "must air" messages. Some possibilities include:

- You were concerned about the people involved and the environment.
- You acted responsibly.
- You cooperated with appropriate authorities.
- Your staff reacted promptly according to a pre-arranged plan.
- Although frightening or upsetting, no serious damage was done outside the organization.
- You are taking steps to prevent a recurrence.

Your messages will obviously depend upon the situation. Look back over Chapter 13 and see if some of the "10 C's of Good Crisis Communications" provide some ideas. You may be tempted to emphasize more than three, but be very careful. You don't want to overwhelm your audience. If you do, they might forget *everything* you say. Make sure, in conversations within your CMT, that you've come up with THE most important issues. No matter what else gets on the TV clip or is published in the newspaper, at least one of these messages must see air time or ink.

Helping Your "Must Air" Messages Get Noticed

Here are two techniques you can use:

(1) *Repeat them frequently.* It has often been said that people need to hear things seven times before they can remember them. It usually feels awkward saying the same thing over and over. However, the newspaper reporter will only print it once and the TV news editor will choose the best "sound bite" to use. Of course you will want to figure out various ways to convey each "must air" message so that you don't sound like a broken record. But don't worry too much about the reporter. Your real audience is the viewer or reader, who will only hear your major point one time.

(2) *Learn the technique of "bridging."* A bridge is a verbal way to get from the question asked to the "must air" message you want to make. (Political consultants call this: "staying on message.") Sometimes the bridges are easy to make. At other times, it takes real creativity.

I'm sure you have all heard ineffective bridges. A politician has been thoroughly briefed by his staff on a number of hot issues prior to a news conference or debate. Then he gets an unrelated question and responds with, "I'm glad you asked that question about gun control. What we need to remember is that the economy has been in much better shape over the past four years..." People are irritated by such obvious evasion, and they wind up not listening because they are so busy thinking, "He didn't even attempt to answer that question!"

What I am recommending is a much smoother transition. You must make your best effort to answer the question posed. But then, without taking much of a breath, you use a bridge like one of the following:

"While I understand your concerns about...we can't lose sight of the fact that ..." or

"Our real focus in dealing with this situation is ..." or

"I believe the main issue here is ..." or

"What I think people need to understand is..."

"Even more to the point is..."

The Importance of Communicating "Must Air" Messages

Too many CEO's and other spokespeople think that the only goal of an interview is to survive. As a matter of fact, an interview should be seen as a positive opportunity. You must take advantage of this chance to provide positive messages! Many times executives will complain that the reporter did not focus on the real issues. Sorry, but a good deal of that responsibility can often be laid at their own feet. Perhaps they were not assertive enough to communicate the "must air" messages. You cannot criticize the reporter if you did not give him the correct information *in a direct and easily quotable way.*

Effective bridging can be difficult, even for professional communicators. It takes practice to do it smoothly. However, it is a very important skill to learn. Skillful application of this technique can help you take a negative question and turn it into a statement that reflects positively on your organization.

"*The situation is so catastrophic that we are devoting all our power to this. But there is no reason to worry.*"

Written in an Opinion Editorial piece by British Prime Minister Tony Blair when discussing the foot-and-mouth disease problem in Europe.

20

"Sound Bites": The Key to Memorable Messages

Y ou were masterful in the way you explained what technical-ly occurred in your crisis situation. Your presentation was thorough. You were quite pleased with the way things went. However, ten minutes after people have turned off the TV or put down the newspaper, if they cannot recall anything that you said, have you really achieved your goal?

You need to spend time making your messages memorable. You need to develop "sound bites" that will stick with your audience.

Helpful Hints to Make Your Messages Memorable

(1) *Analogies*: Let's face it, the regulations surrounding banking and tax laws are overwhelming to the average customer. Procedures followed in hospitals and nursing homes sometimes seem incomprehensible to the patient or his family. Explanations of methods to measure or mediate groundwater contamination are, by nature, quite technical and therefore confusing to a layperson.

Here is how the company I worked for handled an issue of groundwater contamination. Instead of presenting a complex chart showing the details of how a "pump and treat" operation works to clean up a contaminated site, we had a vastly simplified version drawn up. Then our president used it to describe, in simple terms, how it operated. It went like this:

"Imagine that this whole area of contaminated groundwater is like melted, mushy ice cream in a cereal bowl. We have identified that the highest concentration of contamination is in this spot, here in the center of the bowl. What we have proposed doing is to sink a well (represented by this plastic straw I'm inserting) right into this center spot. We would pump the groundwater out of this area just like we could suck on the straw. The contaminated groundwater (or melted ice cream) would be removed. In our operation, it would be passed through drums of activated charcoal to remove the contaminants. The main point is this: Through this process, the suction applied in the center acts to pull the ice cream away from the edges of the bowl. So instead of continuing to migrate off our site, the contamination is being pulled toward the center (the straw) and confined to our property. We can all be assured that no groundwater contamination is spreading to threaten anything in the vicinity."

Such a simple but clear description of a technical process can be pictured, grasped, remembered and probably even believed by the majority of your audience.

This is the power of drawing a mental picture for someone through analogy. Use things people are familiar with in their everyday lives—a car, a heating/air conditioning system, your favorite dessert, etc.

(2) *Illustrations*: The same principles apply here. Give people something with which they can identify to help explain a phenomenon that seems scary. One of the most frequently misunderstood aspects of our company's operation related to the "smoke and

pollution" that always could be seen coming from our facility. Describing our manufacturing processes in technical terms to explain why the public could see steam coming off of our cooling towers and other process equipment usually did not make much of an impression. When I thought to relate it to the fact that you can see steam condensing in the air of a kitchen when you heat up a tea kettle on the stove, I could physically see the light dawn in the eyes of the people to whom I was talking. Suddenly our operations were a lot less frightening.

When I first went to work for the chemical manufacturer in town, the President asked me what rumors I had heard about the company. I told him that one of the most well-known "facts" was that the company saved up all of the "methylethyl bad stuff" that they manufactured during the day and released it at night. I personally had seen that the plumes of what I assumed to be smoke and pollution coming out of the smokestacks were always more intense late at night.

The President calmly explained that it only appeared that there was more steam at night (and especially in winter) because the air was cooler. The company, he said, operated the same way 24 hours a day, 7 days a week. It looked different at those times in the same way that you can see your breath on a cold winter's day even though you cannot in the summer. Aha! I got it! And I used that illustration many times in the next 16 years. Hopefully, my fellow citizens grasped it well enough so they could share the concept with others.

(3) *Stories*: We have all been lulled to sleep by a boring lecture given by a dry professor covering a complex subject or listened to a minister trying to make an obscure theological point. We weren't really getting it. If the professor or minister told a story

about a person or an animal, however, our attention perked up. We followed the story to the end and suddenly understood the point.

If you take the time in the course of an interview to provide an analogy by filling in the sentence: "It is like…" or relate a story or give an illustration, it is more likely that people will remember what you said.

(4) *Clichés*: In choosing to use a cliché, remember that your chances of making your point will be increased if people are already familiar with the expression. For example, if someone heard the phrase "It ain't over 'til…," they would be able to fill in "the fat lady sings" or "it's over." It doesn't matter whether their frame of reference is Kate Smith or Yogi Berra. The point is they remember "It ain't over 'til…" Think of ways you can fill in the end of that sentence to express your message. "It ain't over 'til we have dug up the last scoop of contaminated soil."

There are innumerable cliches that you can take and alter for your purposes. "Hell hath no fury like…" works for Shakespeare lovers. If you give it some thought, you may be able to come up with an appropriate one that will help you communicate your message.

(5) *One-liners*: Quips like "Some days you're the pigeon; some days you're the statue" are clever and memorable. But I caution my clients about using them in a crisis as they can be perceived as flip. Better to save them for the speech before the local Lions Club.

(6) *Contrasts*: You can often make your point by using a word in two different ways. "It doesn't matter if you do things *right* if they are not the *right* things to do."

(7) *Colorful Descriptions*: Remember that you are trying to draw a

mental picture for your audience, something that will stick in their minds. Can't you just see it when someone says, "It was as noticeable as a big black cockroach on a white satin sheet." Or "We don't want our workers to leave their brains in the glove compartment when they walk through the front doors."

(8) *Absolutes/Superlatives (or Diminutives)*: Remember that the media loves drama because that is what their audiences want. So instead of describing a fire as "big," it is more of a sound bite if the Fire Chief says, "In all of my 25 years on the force, that was the biggest fire I ever saw."

(9) *Package and Bundle*: This is a technique that can be used to try to get the media to report several important points you want to make. You preface your remarks by saying something like: "There are three things that the company is doing about this situation. First .... second.... and third...." Of course you have to be concise in the description of the three things, but you might actually be able to have them all see the light of day.

(10)*Acronyms*: I know I cautioned you earlier about the use of jargon. But what I am talking about here are acronyms that you will fully explain and which are easy to remember. I remember once having someone from a state agency refer to people in a nearby community who suffered from the BANANA syndrome. I asked for an explanation.

He said, "You've heard of NIMBY's, right? They are the 'Not In My Back Yard' folks. Then came the PIISEBY's—those who said 'Put It In Somebody Else's Back Yard.' Now we have the BANANA's—'Build Absolutely Nothing Anywhere Near Anybody!' Because the acronym BANANA stuck in my mind, I am still able, with just a little effort, to reconstruct the whole concept. That's a good memory hook.

Spend the Time Required to Develop Good Sound Bites

Once you've come up with memorable ways of phrasing your message, you have a further challenge. Find ways to condense them into concise "sound bites"—something that is so clever, picturesque, dramatic or powerful that a reporter feels compelled to use your words. "BANANA" qualifies as a sound bite. Many cliches do too.

A sound bite is hard to define. It is the sort of thing you know when you hear. To help you develop your own, spend some time studying others. Next time you watch TV news or an interview on "60 Minutes," pay special attention to the words and phrases used to sum up the stories. When you read newspaper and magazine reports, look for what is in quotation marks and try to figure out why those particular words were highlighted. Was it because it was especially clear and logical or because it was colorful, memorable, or clever?

I can hear you now. "I don't have time for this sort of thing. I just want to tell them what I know and get on with it." If you are able to get your major point into a clever sound bite, the editors will use it. That means your point will get air time or be used as a highlighted quote.

You can be certain your critics will be working hard to come up with a sound bite to describe their viewpoint! Unfortunately, their task is often easier. People who feel like victims are driven by such strong emotions that they use dramatic words without even thinking about it.

Imagine Headlines

One technique to help you compose sound bites is to imagine the headline that you would like to see on this story. This forces you to be concise and to search for powerful words. Use your Crisis Management Team in this effort. If you are fortunate enough to have a communications professional on your staff, call upon their expertise. Four or five heads are better than one. One person's idea may spark someone else's better idea until you end up with a great sound bite.

Resist the temptation to just "tell it like it is" and hope the public gets it. The stakes are high. Clear language that draws a mental picture may mean the difference between getting your message across or being ignored while your critics grab the headlines. It's not easy, but it is definitely worth the effort!

Figure 9

MEDIA INTERVIEW WORKSHEET

OBJECTIVE: (25 words or less)

KEY MESSAGES/LIKELY QUESTIONS	SUPPORTING FACTS	SOUND BITES

Note: Be Sure to Notify Other Important Audiences Besides the Media

- ☐ CORPORATE
- ☐ EMPLOYEES
- ☐ LOCAL ELECTED OFFICIALS
- ☐ REGULATORY AGENCIES

Community & Media Relations

21

Putting It All Together

Perhaps you can remember things more easily if you write them down. I know I can. To organize your thoughts in preparation for a media interview, try using the form shown in Figure 9 on the opposite page.

Let me suggest that you make a half dozen copies of this page right now. Enlarge it on your copier so you have plenty of room to write. Put them in a file folder that you can access quickly when the stuff hits the fan. (A bright red folder in the midst of your manilas perhaps?) Then, while others are working on their assigned tasks, you can use this sheet to plan with a couple of members of the Crisis Management Team what you will say to the media who are about to descend.

Develop an Overall Objective

The first thing you should do is identify your objective. What is the basic message? If the readers or viewers can only remember one overriding theme, what would you want that to be?

In my case, what I needed the public to know most often was that the odorous emission we'd just experienced was not a health threat and that we had taken appropriate steps to stop the release.

Completing this initial step will help you stay focused as you work through the rest of the form.

However, if you find it slows you down too much, go on to the rest of the form and come back to it later. Try to formulate your objective, however, as it will help you remember the major theme that you should be striving to communicate in the interview.

Key Messages/Likely Questions

See Chapters 17 and 18 to remind yourself of what you want to capture here. Remember, no more than three "must air" messages, but jot down as many as you can of the questions you think you might be asked.

Once you've captured the thoughts, spend some time working out the most suitable wording. Try out what you come up with on your Crisis Management Team. Read the answers out loud. If you stumble over the wording, or they don't understand what you mean, re-work it until it is clear. Once you are comfortable with the way it is expressed, memorize the key words. Then repeat them over and over until you can say them easily and with confidence.

Supporting Facts

Include here any of the facts of the situation as you know them. The media won't allow you to simply make statements or answer questions without producing some evidence. What makes you so sure the incident is under control? Are you confident the public can rest assured that the person who robbed your bank or was wandering the halls of your hospital or who committed violence in your workplace is safely in custody? What is the scientific evidence to support your contention that the hazardous material people were exposed to will not have any long-term health effects? Is there a third party source who can vouch for what you are saying?

The Oh, So Difficult Sound Bites

In my own experience, and attested to by the majority of executives who have taken my workshops, coming up with clever sound bites is very difficult.

But let's face it. If, fifteen minutes after the TV news program is over, Mr. Smith cannot tell Mrs. Smith anything that you said, what good is it? All your work at crafting a logical and truthful statement is lost if it can't be recalled. What is especially discouraging is that your critics were probably able much more easily to come up with a negative sound bite that Mr. Smith *can* remember.

I will never forget the time a reporter was doing a series of investigative pieces to get the background (and find out who was to blame) for an inactive hazardous waste site on the back of our company's property. She dug into all kinds of court records and discovered one affidavit where an employee described hazardous waste disposal methods of 40 years ago like this:

> "Back then we'd dump the liquid waste from the process in the lagoon in the back. When there was enough, we'd just light a match and throw it in. It was like Dante's Inferno!"

Is there any doubt in your mind what the headline was in the next day's newspaper? There was a dramatic visual image captured in these words. It was a sound bite that stayed with the public.

My job, as media spokesperson, was to try to counteract this powerful message. I'm pretty sure I failed miserably. All I could do was try to point out that (1) such practices were not illegal or even considered to be unwise back in the 1950's and (2) the way hazardous waste is currently disposed of is vastly different and strictly regulated. No pizazz. Nothing memorable. No way a match for "Dante's Inferno."

If you are fortunate enough to have a public relations or

communications professional on your local or corporate staff, call on them for help. They are usually trained in the area of phrasing complex issues in ways laypeople can understand, and many of them are creative enough to come up with sound bites.

In Chapter 20 I gave you some tips on making your messages memorable. When you get to this third column, flip back to that section and see if you can come up with something. It is hard work, but it is well worth the effort. Your corporate reputation may depend on it!

Take Them or Leave Them?

Participants in my workshops often ask if they can take this worksheet along when they go to a TV interview. Even those used to speaking in public can become flustered when the TV camera starts rolling.

If there is a good likelihood that you will experience a total "brain freeze" if you don't have these notes, I would reluctantly say you can take them. Whatever you do, don't call attention to them. Here are the reasons I would much rather you leave them in your office (or with another member of your staff, off camera):

(1) If you have something like the worksheet in your hands, you will have a tendency to fiddle with it or make noise with it. These things are annoying to the viewer and convey a sense of nervousness that you do not want to portray.

(2) Having to refer to notes during a TV interview reduces the impression that you are both competent and confident.

(3) If you are looking down at your notes while being interviewed on TV, you won't be able to maintain eye contact. That's a major negative. When people don't look you in the eye, you think they are either hiding something or outright lying, right?

This critical aspect of eye contact will be covered in much more detail in Chapters 24 and 25.

The worksheet is not a crutch on which you should lean during an interview. It is, however, an excellent way to help you organize your thoughts prior to the interview. Use it to your advantage.

Wouldn't you prefer to have reporters who are writing about you quoting materials you've developed in a period of calm rather than picking up information from unreliable sources during the crisis?

22

Offering Written Materials

E very organization should have written materials ready for distribution at any time, especially during a crisis. I don't mean here just product lists or specification sheets. (They are fine, but you need to go beyond that.) And I don't mean just corporate annual reports, though they have their place as well.

Well, if I don't mean all of those things, what *do* I mean? You need to offer some basic information about your organization and your place in the local community. For instance:

A General Brochure

It need not be a slick, four-color glossy bound document. The first one I did was an 11 x 17" folded sheet, black and white, line drawings (no photos), copied on the office copier. It may not have won any design awards, but it told people what they wanted to know.

What do the media and the public want to know?

Who You Are
- How long have you been doing business at this location?
- Are you privately owned or part of a large corporation?

- A short history of key events at the site
- How many do you employ?

What You Do at This Site
- Describe your products (not by their scientific names—which in the chemical industry usually sound unfamiliar and very scary). As best as you can, relate your products and processes to the common, everyday products with which consumers can identify. An example would help—like chlorine in bleach, etc.
- Relate other activities that take place there (e.g., research and development, engineering, etc.)

What Issues Are of Most Concern?
- You know these from past experience. What are the most frequent questions citizens ask about you? How much better it is for you to address these concerns proactively. For example, during the year prior to January 1, 2000, how many letters and brochures did you get from your local bank assuring you they were ready for Y2K? When utility rates are rising, bill stuffers tell customers why this has to be instead of simply letting their customer service representatives deal with a lot of angry people who have just opened their bills. In my brochure, I talked about steam clouds perceived as pollution, odors feared as health threats, surface groundwater contamination thought to be threatening public drinking water, and other issues.

Benefits Your Presence Provides to the Community
- Tax payments made to municipalities and schools to reduce the burden on homeowners
- Contributions to local charitable and civic organizations
- Participation of employees in local community organizations

- Stimulation of the local economy through wages and purchases
- Cooperative efforts with local schools

This publication need not be expensive. The main facts could be captured on the front and back of one sheet of paper. But in this day of desktop publishing, you can quite easily put together a presentable tri-fold brochure, complete with photos of your facility and the faces of friendly employees.

You will find these brochures come in handy for lots of purposes. They are a great general information piece suitable for distribution in your lobby, at speaking engagements with local groups, with customers (or those you hope will be customers), students, prospective employees, interested neighbors, and many others. You will wonder how you ever did without it!

It is also an ideal piece to have available for the media. When a crisis has erupted, you won't have time to provide all of this background information to a reporter. It gives them solid information from which to draw when they write their story. Having it in writing—the way you phrased it when you had plenty of time to think it through—gives you a much better chance of having it presented correctly in the media coverage.

Glossary of Terms and Explanations of Technicalities

If your business requires the use of any kind of specialized terminology that might not be readily understood (and there are few that do not!), consider developing a glossary of terms to include in your packet of information.

Put yourselves in the shoes of a member of the general public and listen to how people talk around your workplace. Do you use a lot of abbreviations for regulations and government agencies? Are your products and processes described with technical terms? Would the way you talk pass the "Mama test?" (Would your mother understand what you are talking about?) If not, re-read point 7 in Chapter 13, "Be Clear," and develop a sheet that provides a glossary of terms. It will help the media write their story. You do not want them guessing about what something means.

For those of you familiar with Material Safety Data Sheets (MSDS), how about just giving the public or the media one of them? I can almost hear the shrieks! I could not agree more. MSDS's are *terrible* for the purpose of communicating to the general public. Don't get me wrong. They have their place. Emergency responders may know how to read them for their purposes without going into a total panic. However, members of the general public will usually search through them for something they can understand. "Let's see… hmmmm… LD/50…don't understand… IDLH level… don't understand… lethal dose… A-HA! That I understand! This stuff is going to kill people!"

This is dangerous enough when it's a local citizen. If it's a member of the press, it is *very* dangerous. All kinds of misconceptions can be promulgated by the press and then accepted as true by the public.

Many reporters now know enough to ask for an MSDS. You must have them available. My *strong* suggestion, though, is to also have available what I call laymen's language "Chemical Information Sheets (CIS)."

How are these developed? I'll tell you how we did it. I set up a meeting with our Safety Manager, a Ph.D. scientist from Research & Development, our Environmental Affairs Manager, and myself. Their job was to explain the MSDS to me, the Manager of Public Affairs who came to her job by way of being a Political Science major. (It was not because of my technical skills or my background in science that I was originally hired as the Administrative Assistant to the President.) We would talk together—or, rather, they would talk and I would listen, take copious notes, and try to understand. They had to talk and talk until I was clear about what they meant. Once I was sure I "got it," I would re-write each section of the MSDS in non-technical language and pass it by them to ensure that it was accurate.

We were careful to be true to the facts, but we put things into perspective. For example, we explained how the odors people could notice compared to levels workers were allowed to be exposed to for eight hours a day/forty hours a week. Similarly, we could compare the levels of a substance that would be Immediately Dangerous to Life and Health (IDLH) to the usual levels measured at our fenceline.

The whole process took anywhere between two and three hours each. We did them for the thirteen high volume chemicals which were the most likely to be involved in any kind of incident.

So, while in total it took a full workweek for each of four people, it was time well spent! There were many times when I blessed the day that we decided to undertake this project. Whenever an incident occurred, I was pleased to hear the reporters quoting from our Chemical Information Sheets when explaining about the chemical to the public. When doctors' offices called us on the day a release caused the evacuation of the high school and kids were in their waiting rooms complaining of nausea and headaches, we sent the MSDS sheets they asked for. But we also sent the CIS. The laymen's language description of usual symptoms of exposure and first aid procedures were sufficient for their needs and calmed a lot of anxiety.

Biographies of Key Personnel

Another thing that should be written up is biographical data on the key managers. People will want to know something about the company personnel who are giving them information. The pieces don't have to be long—one to two paragraphs are sufficient. Who is he? What is his position within the organization? Is he a person of authority? What is his background? What qualifies him to be answering questions or managing the crisis?

Include the biographies of those people who would be most likely to comment. Prepare a number of them. Then, depending on the type of crisis, select the relevant bios for the press kit (see next page). Usually, the most senior person in the organization should have his biography included.

Be sure you keep these biographies up to date with at least an annual review. People increase their level of education, get promotions, volunteer to serve on new Boards of Directors in the community, etc., and you want to stay on top of these developments.

Visual/Graphical Material

Simple graphics or photographs often explain things more clearly than anything else does. Think about what would be useful for your organization. How about:

- a simplified flow chart explaining your manufacturing process in non-proprietary terms, a systems diagram explaining the steps in how a check clears in a bank, or how a power grid works

- an organization chart describing complex reporting relationships

- an overhead photo of your facility so you could point out where the fire is, where fire trucks are stationed, where the closest neighbors live, etc.

Use your imagination. What kind of picture would be worth a thousand words when trying to describe what you do and what is happening in this crisis?

Building a Press Kit

All of the items mentioned above should be put into folders in *two* easily accessible places (in case one is out of commission because of the incident). The person designated to meet with the media can go to one of these spots and put together a "press kit." This doesn't need to be fancy. A manila folder will do. The employee just pulls out the general brochure, the annual report and product information, the glossary of terms (or a Chemical Information Sheet if applicable), the biographical data of the key personnel who will probably be addressing the issue, and any pertinent visual/graphical data. This can then be given to the media while they are waiting to be briefed.

Then all that needs to be added when it is prepared is...

A Statement About the Current Incident

I highly recommend that you provide this even if you already provided an oral statement to the radio station, the TV news crew and the newspaper reporter. There are several reasons for this:

(1) Writing it down helps clarify the issues as you work with the Crisis Management Team;

(2) Writing it down may help ingrain the ideas in the spokesperson's mind so she is more apt to remember the main points when answering the reporter's questions;

(3) If a crisis goes on for many hours so that there needs to be a change in spokesperson, it will be obvious what has already been communicated.

Hand the reporters your statement in person or fax or e-mail it to their offices. This minimizes the chances of being misquoted.

Remember, though, just because you have a written statement that you worked out with your Crisis Management Team does not mean that you should *read* it. The impact of your remarks is drastically reduced if you are looking down to read the material instead of looking the reporter in the eye. Your credibility, and that of your organization, is at stake. (See Chapter 25 for more details on body language.)

The Value of Being Prepared Ahead of Time

There is no way that you will have enough time during the heat of battle to prepare all of the materials which have been mentioned here. You are lucky if you have the time to put together a good statement about the current incident. Having all of the background information at your fingertips will prove very helpful to the media. They will appreciate it and respect you for having it done. These positive impressions may well find their way into this news report and enhance your reputation in their eyes for future stories as well.

Avoiding Reporter Tricks and Traps

During an interview, you may find yourself confronted with one or more of the following reporter tricks. Be on your guard, because if you fall into one of these traps, you will not be happy with the outcome.

The Reporter Uses Negative Words in the Question

It is vital that you remember that, in most interviews (except when you are "live" in a breaking story or on a talk show), the reporter's question will not be heard or read by the audience. They are just trying to get you to deliver a quotable quote that will then become the organization's response. So you want to be sure you do not repeat negative words that the reporter uses.

The reporter may use the words "sloppy procedures" or "negligence" when referring to an industrial accident. Perhaps the reporter refers to a "callous attitude" of hospitals or nursing homes to their patients. He may state that the line technicians for the telephone company are "obviously incompetent" to handle the breakdown in the communications system. My favorite was when a chemical industry executive was asked, "Are you still burying all of your chemical garbage in that cesspool behind the plant?"

Your natural inclination, especially when you are righteously indignant, is to emphatically deny the charge.

"We do NOT have sloppy procedures in our company."

"We are by no means negligent."

"None of us have a callous attitude toward our patients."

"Our workers are not incompetent!"

"It is not true that we are burying chemical garbage in a cesspool behind our plant!"

If you simply put a "no" or a "not" in your answer, LOOK OUT! You are not successfully refuting the charge. Instead, you have reinforced the association of these negatives with your organization. It is infinitely better to not use the negatives; instead, turn them into positives by saying:

"Our procedures are very clear on this matter and our employees are trained regularly on how to execute them."

"Our employees are extremely conscientious and take tremendous pride in the way they carry out their responsibilities."

"The physical, mental, and emotional well-being of our patients is the primary concern of our institution."

"Our line technicians are highly trained and their capabilities have been proven under these very trying circumstances."

"I believe what you are asking about is our system for handling hazardous waste on our site. We have an excellent program. Let me tell you about it..."

When the Question is Hostile, Use the DAM Principle

I know, I know. You're spelling that word another way! What it stands for here is:

Defuse the bomb: Exert as much self-control as you can muster. The question may be hostile, but you must tell yourself that it is not directed at you personally. Sift through the hostility to get to the real issue.

Answer the question: Use the advice provided earlier to formulate a clear, concise, positive answer, hopefully with a quotable sound bite.

Make your point: Remember to bridge to one of your "must air" messages. Every question posed to you, regardless of the level of hostility, can provide you with an opportunity to reinforce your major points.

If a False Assertion is Made, Correct It

Whether intentionally or not, reporters will often ask a question that is based on an inaccurate premise. "Employees of your company have been guilty of sexual harassment on several occasions, so what do you have to say this time?" If you let that first part of the question go unchallenged, your audience will assume that it is true, whether they remember hearing anything about the cases or not. Before answering the question, you should say, "First let me set the record straight. Allegations that were brought against two of our employees last year were later proven in court to be totally unfounded and were dropped. As to this current allegation...." I realize that I am advocating here that you bring up something negative, but it must be obvious to you that the reporter will write about the previous cases in this article to show a history, so you must be very definite in refuting this.

The Reporter Poses a Multi-Faceted Question

It seems overwhelming when the questions come rapid fire in one long breath. "When was the last time your nursing home was found guilty of deficiencies like this one during state inspections and how many violations were there, for what, and what did you do about it?" It can be very confusing for the person being interviewed. Do you have to take them one by one as they were posed? Do you have to answer them all? How can you even be expected to **remember** them all?

My advice is to pick out the one question for which you have the best answer and respond to it. Then stop. One of two things will happen. The reporter may just go on to the next question because you have been responsive in some way. Or he may say, "What about ..." and repeat one of the other parts of the question. That's fine— at least you've had a little more time to think about how you want to respond.

Confusing Questions Should Be Clarified

A reporter does not always ask clear questions. He may be legitimately confused. Sometimes, asking fuzzy questions is intentional. He may hint at something without asking a specific question to see if you will take him into other subjects of interest. In your sessions with the Crisis Management Team, you were supposed to have thought of the most likely questions. You were even advised to think of the "Oh, s—t!" question you hoped would not be asked. Now the reporter seems to be alluding to the very topic you wanted to avoid.

Before you stray unnecessarily into a huge mine field, just ask the reporter to repeat the question. Saying, "I'm sorry. I don't understand what you are asking," is perfectly acceptable. Get the reporter to rephrase the question or give additional information. There are good reasons to do this: (1) You may avoid opening a Pandora's box of additional issues the reporter did not know enough to ask about, and (2) It gives you some additional time to think. (At times like this, every little bit helps!)

Of course, you can overuse this technique. If you ask for repetition of every question, the reporter will quickly assume that you are either stalling, or you're very dumb! However, when you truly do not understand the question, you have every right to ask for clarification.

Don't Let the Reporter Put Words in Your Mouth

This one is akin to setting false assertions straight. It happens this way. The reporter asks you a question. You answer it. Then he says, "So what you are saying is ...." and proceeds to state something that is not true or is a misinterpretation of what you had said. Once again, you must immediately set this straight. You have to overcome your desire to say, "No, stupid! That's not what I said at all." This is a time for you to swallow your pride and say, "Apparently I did not express myself as clearly as I wanted. What I meant to convey was..."

Do You Believe the Reporter if He Says It's "Off the Record?"

To be safe, the best rule is to NEVER say anything to a reporter that you would not want to see repeated in the media. Remember when Connie Chung said to Newt Gingrich's mother, "Just whisper in my ear, dear, what DO they call Hillary on the Hill?" Poor Mrs. Gingrich, who did not have much experience dealing with the media, may have taken that as a sort of promise that Connie Chung would not trumpet what she said all over the place. But Chung did, and it caused acute embarrassment to Mrs. Gingrich's son.

If you are a communications professional who has a great deal of experience with the media, you **might** be able to work in this arena. It usually requires a long-standing relationship based on mutual trust and respect between the reporter and the spokesperson who knows the difference between terms like "off the record," "not for attribution," "background" and "check with me." Even then, it can be tricky. Public relations professionals have sometimes been burned when a reporter has felt that the information he has gotten is in the public interest or just too juicy to ignore. To be safe, just assume that there is no such thing as "off the record."

Avoid the Blame Game

When something has gone wrong, reporters want to know who is to blame. Which employee made the mistake that caused the accident? Who is the manager who let things get into such a sorry state that a regulatory agency has cited you for serious violations? Who is responsible for not enforcing the policy that resulted in a serious incident? They will press for an answer.

For legal reasons, as well as in the interest of fairness and not judging before all the facts are in, you do not want to assign blame. People who are initially thought to be at fault can later be found innocent and you will have besmirched their name—obvious grounds for a lawsuit. Your lawyers also do not want you to assign blame because of the liability implications.

If it appears very likely that a member or members of your organization are responsible for causing an incident, you can move cautiously to help resolve the problem without publicly pointing fingers. While the cause of the situation is being investigated, which may take some time, you could offer to do what you can to help solve the problems, acting as a good corporate citizen.

Don't Fall for the "Open Mike" Trick

Interviews for television sometimes end up this way. The reporter, who has been passing the microphone back and forth between you and him, just leaves the microphone in front of you and is silent. As the silence lengthens, you tend to become uncomfortable, thinking that you must say something else. You know TV shows cannot abide "dead air." You feel compelled to fill the vacuum. In your nervousness, you say something else. The reporter has just tricked you into opening a whole new line of questioning.

Realize right up front that you are NOT responsible for "dead air." The station will not allow it. They just will not use that part of the interview. The reporter wanted to see if you would give him anything else he can use. Instead of launching into another subject, you should just wait a sufficient amount of time, smile slightly, and say, "Is there anything else?" Better still, you can use that time to try to emphasize one of your major messages again. "I just want to be sure that the public understands...."

This is a good place to also remind you to assume that every microphone you see is "live." (There may even be some you can't see!) Remember the embarrassing incident when candidate George W. Bush was caught calling a highly respected reporter a nasty name? The press played that clip over and over. Be careful what you say in any public setting, even under your breath. You never know who is listening—or recording!

Never Lose Your "Cool"

Any one of the tricky techniques described above could be enough to make you angry. If the reporter uses a lot of them, you are bound to feel your blood pressure rising. Be very careful. It never pays to lose your temper with the media.

Remember that they are actively searching for controversy, drama and conflict. They realize that, if they drive you to the limit of your patience, you may blurt out something they can use to spice up their report. But this is NOT the kind of attention you want for yourself or your organization.

If you remain calm, even under difficult circumstances, your audience—and even the reporter—will respect you a great deal more. Having their respect is worth the energy spent foregoing your intense desire to wring the reporter's neck!

Know a Recording Device Can Always be "On"

Whenever a reporter is in your area, beware of everything you do and say even if you don't see any equipment—they are easily hidden. Examples abound of public figures severely embarrassed to hear their words, which they thought were whispered only to a colleague, played out publicly.

You must also guard against inappropriate facial expressions and gestures. An example of the former: Bill Clinton was marching in a funeral procession for Transportation Secretary Ron Brown. In one off-guard moment, the President laughed and smiled widely. As soon as he caught a glimpse of the TV camera, he resumed a somber expression. Too late! That clip became part of the evening news.

An even more subtle reporter trick is to film the spokesperson in a pre-interview "warm-up" period and then use just the video portion while the anchorperson does a voice-over. One emergency management spokesperson I know was talking in a "warm-up" about the previous evening's exciting baseball game. How distressed she was to see herself on the news that night with some very agitated gestures when the anchor was talking about whether there was really a crack in the near-by dam! Since it is true that body language communicates more powerfully than words (see the next section), her audio message, "Everything is fine!" was overpowered by the video message.

VI

Never Underestimate the Power of Body Language

*Planning **what** you are going to say is very important. But you need to have an appreciation for the vital importance of **how** you say it! Whether your messages are really heard and, more importantly, believed depends heavily on your body language.*

Your body language speaks so loudly,
people cannot hear what your words are saying.

What Is Body Language?

Back in the 1980's I heard someone use the term "neurolin-guistic programming." I had no idea what they were talking about. I came to find out that a lot of NLP has to do with the concept of "body language."

I want to take a few minutes to make sure you all understand it the same way I do. When I am finished, I hope you will realize that HOW something is said usually vastly overpowers WHAT is said.

Anyone who is communicating with an audience, whether in person or through a TV interview, must pay a great deal of attention to body language and master its intricacies.

The Essence of Body Language

You witness communication through body language every day. At home, conversations with spouses or teenagers often include things like:

> "LOOK at me when I'm talking to you!"
>
> "Don't you roll those eyes at me!"
>
> "I don't like that tone of voice."

When someone is making a presentation at a meeting and his voice is weak or he mumbles or reads the entire presentation, you are less than impressed.

Law enforcement personnel go through extensive training in body language. That's because it has been proven that they can learn whether a suspect is lying from things he does with his body during questioning.

Body language has to do with:
- the confidence level exhibited
- hand gestures
- shuffling of feet or swaying
- tone and pace of the voice
- facial expressions
- eye contact

In the next chapter, I will deal with the specific things you should do as well as those things to avoid. But first, I want to present some evidence of just how important it is to master good body language techniques.

The Importance of Body Language

When I first became aware of body language, like many people, I went a bit overboard. Sitting in staff meetings after reading an article on it, I'd lose track of what was being said. I was too busy trying to figure out why people were sitting with their arms crossed over their chest; noticing who was leaning which way; trying to remember what it supposedly meant when a person was looking over my left shoulder when I spoke, etc. I was just about to give up on the whole subject when I read that an important university study by Professor Albert Mehrabian had been done and replicated several times since. The study is summarized with this chart, shown in Figure 10, which speaks volumes.

Figure 10

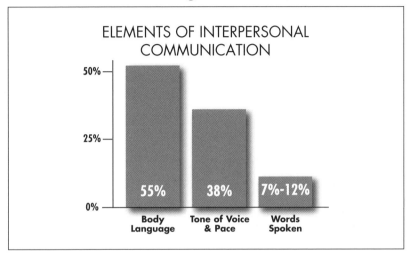

What this demonstrates is that the message communicated to your audiences comes across to them from three things:

(1) *The Actual Words You Say*

Even just a few minutes after a message has been communicated, the impression that a listener or a TV viewer has of that message is based only 7-12% on the actual words you said! Yes, even after you and your Crisis Management Team worked so hard to come up with exactly the right words to communicate your "must air" messages or answer the most likely questions, it's only 7-12% of what people remember.

(2) *The Tone and Pace of Your Voice*

The study also shows that 33-38% of your message is communicated to them by the tone and pace of your voice. You can prove this to yourself with just a few exercises. The next time you and your spouse or child have a misunderstanding, try saying, "Well, I'm sorr-ee!" in a sarcastic tone of voice. Just watch the flames get hotter. Alternatively, say it like you **really** are sorry. See if the problem doesn't start to get solved right then.

Another aspect to tone of voice has to do with the words you tend to emphasize. It is important to pay attention to this. For example, read out loud these five sentences, each time emphasizing the word in bold typeface.

> **I** didn't say you were stupid.
>
> I didn't **say** you were stupid.
>
> I didn't say **you** were stupid.
>
> I didn't say you **were** stupid.
>
> I didn't say you were **stupid**.

See what I mean? The exact same words convey five different meanings depending on the emphasis given a word. This exercise also demonstrates how it is very possible that a person's statement can be interpreted many different ways depending on the voice inflection.

(3) *Body Language*

> This then leaves a whopping 55% of your message that depends on things you do or don't do with your body. Your listeners may not be able to verbalize this. However, their subconscious mind is picking up these vibrations and they are definitely affecting how you (and your organization) are perceived.

One Important Note

I'll be concentrating on helping you give a good TV interview. But remember two things:

(1) Reporters for newspapers are very conscious of body language too. If it's a telephone interview, they will only have the tone and pace of your voice to help them judge your sincerity, nervousness over the situation, etc. But if a reporter is at your site for a face-to-face interview, he will be taking it all in and making judgments based on what he reads in your body language.

(2) People attending a public meeting will be swayed mightily by the messages you are communicating subliminally through your body language. TV cameras may also be at these meetings, especially if you are being called "on the carpet" to explain why an incident occurred.

Pay Attention to This Important Aspect of Communicating

Hundreds of years ago, Voltaire said: "Men...employ speech only to conceal their thoughts." Body language either supports your words or contradicts them. A case in point: try saying out loud "I'm not mad at you" in a soft tone of voice with your arms open and hands outstretched to someone with a warm expression on your face. Then try saying "I'm NOT mad at you!" through clenched teeth and with a glaring expression while your arms are folded across your chest. See what I mean?

In the next chapter I'll provide some specific guidance in how to use these elements of body language to your advantage.

Whether people like you and trust you determines whether they believe the risks to which you expose them are acceptable or not."

—Noel Griese, Crisis Research Council

CHAPTER
25

If It's Not For You,
It's Against You

Proper use of body language can reinforce your messages and convince the public, through the media, that you are trying to do the right thing. Improperly used, it will either detract from or contradict your verbal messages. Tone of voice was covered in the last chapter. Here we will concentrate on what to do with your feet, hands, and face.

Control Your Feet

Have you ever watched someone giving a presentation who cannot seem to hold still? He is either shuffling his feet or frequently shifting his weight from one foot to the other. What message do you get right away from this fidgeting? Very often the thought crosses your mind, either consciously or unconsciously, "I wonder what he is so nervous about?" You begin to wonder if you can trust what he is saying. If he were telling the truth, why would he be so nervous?

Another thing that nervous people do is sway from side to side. Let's assume that you *are* nervous. (Who among us isn't at least a bit nervous when the TV lights go on? You can't help but think that your every word and gesture is being captured on film for posterity and for your employees, your site neighbors, your competitors and your mother-in-law to see.) If you are standing with your feet parallel to each other and spread shoulder width apart, you may well find yourself swaying back and forth. It's a soothing thing to do—like the motion often used when trying to calm a cranky baby. In this case, it's the baby inside you that wants the interview to be over! How annoying this is for people to see when they are trying to listen to you. They find that they cannot give your message the attention it deserves when your swaying distracts them. All they can think about is when you are going to stop.

My advice is to place one foot just slightly ahead of the other, close together. Bend your knees just a little to relax yourself. In this position you can't sway or you'll just fall right over—that would look great on TV!

Use Your Hands Judiciously

People always want to know what to do with their hands when they are talking. None of these positions feels completely comfortable:

- "Standing at Attention" with both hands ramrod stiff at your sides
- "At Ease" with hands clasped behind your back
- "Protection Against the Direct Kick in Soccer" also known as the "Fig Leaf"
- "Praying" with hands clasped and knuckles turning white

Any of the above hand positions can be okay for part of the interview. You just don't want to stay in one position all of the time. It makes you look stiff and uncomfortable.

Using your hands to make small appropriate gestures to emphasize your words is ideal. If you are the type of person who uses your hands the whole time you talk, that will become a distraction to your listener. Just try to tone it down. If you are saying, "The organization is going to do three things as we move forward to solve this crisis," you can use your fingers to tick off the three things. Your goal is to look as natural and relaxed as possible.

It is understandable that you will be tense during an interview. The adrenaline is pumping and butterflies may be noticeable in your stomach. Adrenaline is a good thing. It provides that energy level you need and shows people that you are actively involved in responding to the crisis. The trick is to control the energy and get the butterflies to fly in formation. When some of this nervous energy can be released through small, appropriate gestures with your hands, then it doesn't come out in other ways, such as having your hands or voice shake.

What is natural for me is to clasp my hands gently at about waist height. Then, when I want to make a gesture, it can be accomplished easily before returning to this basic stance. Some people prefer to keep one hand in a suit pocket for a good deal of the time. That leaves your other hand free for the gestures. Do what is most natural for you, but try to vary it occasionally

Whatever you do, make sure you do not have any annoying habits with your hands. You may not even be aware of them unless you have been videotaped while giving a presentation or have a good friend or colleague who will tell you about it. What are some of these annoying habits?

- Women fiddling with their hair
- Men jingling the change in their pocket
- Women playing with their jewelry
- Anyone who touches the face a lot, whether pulling ears, rubbing a beard, or touching your nose. (Be especially careful if you

are a nose toucher! An astute observer of body language once told me that usually means the speaker is actually thinking, "Boy, this really stinks! Even I don't believe what I'm telling them!")

Your Face

Oh, how we communicate with facial expressions! They are visible for everyone to see before we are even conscious of them. In less than a second, we can have a look come to our face that shows pleasure, disgust, surprise, contempt, or anger. We may move quickly to try to say something, but our true feelings have been communicated through a facial expression. Make no mistake. Your audience will be searching your face for clues as to whether they can believe you or not. Do you look sincere? Do you show concern about the incident? Do you seem to care about the people involved?

It is a real skill to be able to control facial expressions. It can only be done if you are extremely conscious of trying to maintain an even, open and warm expression at all times.

The Eyes Have It

What do they have? The key to whether your message is accepted by the audience. It is difficult to overemphasize just how important it is to maintain eye contact with those to whom you are speaking.

I'm sure you already know that it is important to look someone in the eye when you are talking. If you were to interview someone for a job and she couldn't look you in the eye, you would immediately assume that she was not being honest or was hiding something. If a person's eyes were darting all over the place, your subconscious would quickly grasp that the person was shifty and not to be trusted.

If human resource professionals and law enforcement officers are taught not to believe these people's words, why should the public believe you if you don't look them in the eye?

When you are talking to a TV reporter, you have to be very conscious of certain things related to eye contact. In my experience, when a single TV reporter was interviewing me, he would line himself up facing me with the camera stationed over his shoulder. In this way, by talking with him, it would be picked up as my looking almost into the camera. (You don't want to *actually* look into the camera, as that looks hokey from people's living rooms.) You want to have a conversation with the reporter.

The trick is to KEEP YOUR EYES ON THE REPORTER'S EYES AT ALL TIMES—OR WHERE THE REPORTER'S EYES WOULD BE IF HE WERE LOOKING AT YOU.

Although you will be sorely tempted, especially while trying to gather your thoughts to answer a question, do not allow yourself to:

- look down (like hoping that a big hole would suddenly open and swallow you up)

- look up to the ceiling (as if praying for a greater power to come down and save you)

- close your eyes for long periods of time (make it go away!)

- blink furiously (don't hurt me).

All of these things communicate nervousness and lack of confidence. You look either shifty or like you are hooding your eyes, so you are not going to be believed.

As I am telling you this, I realize how hard this is to do. It is not natural to stare at people this way. In fact, I'm sure your mother taught you that it was rude. In this instance, I am telling you, "Forget what your mother told you!" You MUST keep eye contact. Not the Darth Vader stare where you attempt to intimidate the reporter. And not the wide-eyed vacant stare that tells them "The lights are on but nobody's home." You want to make and keep a visual connection with the reporter—and therefore his audience tuning in at home. It lets everyone know that you are paying attention, are concerned about the situation, and will be answering the questions as best you can.

Videotape Yourself in Practice Sessions

The best thing you can do to check out how you rate in the area of body language is to have yourself videotaped. This can be done as you give a normal prepared speech within your organization or as you role-play a media interview during a mock crisis.

The camera doesn't lie, even if your colleagues are too hesitant to point out some annoying habits or lack of eye contact. Review the film in the privacy of your own home if you wish. Get family members to critique it. (They are usually only too glad to give honest feedback!) You will see the areas that you need to work on to help make sure that your body language supports your message and does not detract from it.

Since more than half of your message is communicated by the way you use body language, it is well worth your efforts to improve in this area. Only practice can bring improvement, so get started!

SECTION
VII

Concluding Thoughts

You have done the best you could. Now you wait to see how the media treats you. You try to get back on an even footing with the community. You hope you learned from your experiences so things will go better next time

Next time? Yes, there's apt to be a next time. Follow the recommendations here to practice, through realistic role-plays, to make your response even more effective than it was this time.

"Sometimes (the sportswriters) write what I say and not what I mean."

—Pedro Guerrero, St. Louis Cardinals.

CHAPTER

26

Considering Your Options if Misquoted or Maligned

L et's say you have followed all my advice. Does this mean you will love the evening TV news broadcast or the story in the next morning's paper? Of course not.

You have to be realistic. The media is not in the business of making you look good. You are not paying their salary, so don't expect the story to read like it would have if your Public Relations staff had written it!

There is always the chance that you have run up against a journalist or an editor who cares more about gaining an audience than sticking to journalistic ethics. Or perhaps one of them has had a past encounter with you or your organization that left them angry. Maybe they distrust your entire industry. These things do happen.

More likely, however, an inaccurate story was caused by other reasons. We can examine some of them here and think about whether there was anything you could have done differently.

Some Things That Could Have Gone Wrong

(1) *You were misquoted.* Did you give the reporter your statement in writing? Did you jargon-proof your statement? Did you spend enough time planning exactly what you were going to say to

make sure it was clear? (Or, were you like Pedro Guerrero of the St. Louis Cardinals who complained about the sportswriters who covered him, "Sometimes they write what I say and not what I mean.") Did you make your statement pass the "Mama test?" (That is, if you used those words to explain the situation to your own mother would she understand it?) If you didn't spend enough time making sure that the reporter had sufficient background to grasp the situation, you cannot be too surprised to have been misquoted.

(2) *You were taken out of context.* If the reporter quoted one part of your statement which ended up giving an unclear or untrue impression, maybe it was because you didn't provide the necessary information succinctly enough. Especially in television reports, you only have a few seconds to make your case (30 seconds, perhaps, in a small town cable news show where whole stories are 2-3 minutes in length; 7 seconds in a large metropolitan area where there is even more news to cram in). If you don't practice capturing your major messages in sound bites, you are practically inviting the editors to take a hatchet to your remarks. You usually won't like the results. As Ralph Waldo Emerson said once, "Spartans, stoics, heroes, saints and gods use a short and powerful speech."

(3) *You were portrayed as the "black hat."* If you feel you were made to look bad, you must truthfully assess how you handled the whole interview process.

- Did you indicate early on that you planned to cooperate with the media or did you make them work hard to hunt you down and extract a statement?

- Did you do what you could to help the reporter? Did you provide him with access to the people he needed to talk to?

Were you considerate of his deadlines? Did you give him background information that would allow him to learn quickly about the subject (without overwhelming him with detail)? Did you make it as non-technical as possible?

- Did you treat him with respect and assume that he would act with journalistic ethics or did your negative attitude put him off right away?

What Do You Do Now?

Regardless of the reasons for your displeasure, the question now becomes: what do you do about it?

(1) *Assess the Seriousness of the Impact.* Just because the report did not come out the way you liked, it does not mean that you should make an issue of it. You must get some objective assessments of the story's impact. Find out what impression it made on your important audiences.

- Do some informal polling of your employees. If they are concerned about something in the news report, you can address it directly with them. Post the newspaper article on the bulletin boards (physical or electronic), highlight the areas of concern, and provide corrections or clarifications.

- Have the person who has the best channel of communication speak with local elected officials and bring up the subject to see if there is a reaction. If there is an issue that needs to be addressed, you can do so immediately, before the misinformation spreads further.

- Get the sales and marketing staff to check in with some key customers (if this is other than a purely local story) to gauge whether there needs to be further communication with them.

- Ask your spouse or close personal friends what is being said in the community. Make sure you and your employees continue to attend local civic and community meetings. If you appear to be hiding, it will seem that you are feeling guilty about something. In your conversations with people, you will quickly get a sense for just how serious the impact was on your corporate reputation. Are they joking with you about it being your company's "turn in the barrel" or are they asking serious questions that indicate true community concern?

After taking the pulse in this way, you can better judge what you need to do.

(2) *Consider Your Options.* You actually have a wide range including:

- *Do Nothing.* This is certainly the correct choice in many cases. Your informal surveys as described above may reveal no serious damage. If minor points need to be clarified, it can be done in a low-key way either verbally or in writing, and aimed specifically at the affected audience. As far as the newspaper or TV station is concerned, sometimes you are better off simply ignoring them rather than running the risk of drawing more attention to yourself. You don't want to be portrayed as a whiner.

- *Speak to the Reporter.* If the reporter did a decent job of covering the subject, especially if it was a complex issue, I always thought it was a good move to call and let them know that. Once this had been said, the reporter seemed more inclined to listen when I pointed out a place where something had gone awry. If the point in question is one that is likely to appear again in future stories, I asked that a "note to the record" be made.

  Newspapers keep archived copies of their stories. When a reporter is assigned a story, he will often go back and see what has been written previously. A "note to the record" should prevent the same mistake from being made again.

- *Speak to the Reporter's Boss.* When you speak first to the reporter, you may find that he is unconcerned about his slanted reporting (or even his failure to contact you for your side of the story). If that is the case, you may need to go to the editor or regional bureau head. When you talk to this individual, you have to be very clear just why you feel you have a legitimate complaint. Be specific. Stay calm and professional. Indicate that you want to continue to work with them but that you expect to be treated fairly. Most of the time, this is enough. You don't need to threaten to pull your firm's advertising. Journalists do not respond positively to that tactic. In fact, it often backfires.

Only once in 16 years as spokesperson did I ever have to get really confrontational with an Editor. A reporter—apparently intent on winning a journalistic award for investigative reporting—systematically ignored the background information I gave her to help put an issue into perspective. She insisted on reporting on a situation in the most sensationalistic terms she could muster. Several conversations with her about this elicited what seemed to be sincere, sweet apologies—followed by the exact same treatment the next day! Our corporate management team was becoming extremely leery of continuing to provide her with ANY information. After this happened for the third time, I telephoned her editor. My message was simple: We have tried to cooperate, as is our policy. However, if the newspaper wanted to have future comments on this issue, they would have to send a different reporter. They did.

At other times, it was the reporter's boss (the editor) who was the problem! He had had bad experiences with company spokespersons before I took the job; that attitude was very hard to change. When that is the case, you have to use other avenues to get your point across.

• *Ask for a printed correction.* Sometimes the negative impression that has been made on the public by a news story is so damaging that you feel you simply must address it in writing. If you can convince the editor that something inaccurate was written, you can request the matter be addressed in the special section of the newspaper set aside for corrections.

Of course it is in small type and not nearly as dramatic as the major story with 32 point headlines where the false statement was made, but it is often better than nothing. (There may be more people like me who always flip to that page of the newspaper first.) You just have to realize when you ask for a correction that you will be keeping the story alive for one more day. Those who didn't read the bad stuff about you on Monday would have it called to their attention on Tuesday.

• *Write a Letter to the Editor.* If the issue has a relatively high visibility, either because the editors gave it major play or have done a series of stories on it, you may need to tell your side of the story in this way. You don't whine and attack the reporter. You simply set the record straight factually, using a moderate tone.

Most people tend to read the Letters to the Editor because that is where the controversial issues are covered. Many who read the original article might have wondered if you would respond or if they'd be left with just one side of the story.

Just realize that, if you write a Letter to the Editor, you are inviting retaliation by groups that were happy to see negative things written about you. You may prolong the controversy. And you may alienate the reporter who will now be more anxious to report on any future misfortunes or allegations of wrongdoing.

- *Write an Opinion Editorial (OpEd) Piece.* This takes things a step beyond the Letter to the Editor. OpEd pieces are usually longer, often with an accompanying photo. It is placed prominently in the editorial section. The writer may be the CEO himself. An OpEd piece is usually called for only when there has been either a serious misstatement of facts or a series of negatively slanted articles that have left a damaging black mark against the reputation of your organization.

  Remember those people in the middle of the bell curve in Chapter 10? The Sympathizers, the Straddlers, and the Skeptics are *waiting* for you to speak up and defend yourself. If you do not provide information to counteract the negative reporting, people will have no choice but to believe what they have read. And your Supporters won't have any ammunition with which to defend you.

  True, you probably won't convince the Splenetics, but that should not be what motivates you to communicate in this way anyway. Writing an OpEd piece may even motivate some Splenetics to write a Letter to the Editor about you — or an OpEd piece of their own. However, these disadvantages are usually outweighed by the advantages of providing the majority of the public with the information they need so they can make up their own minds intelligently.

- *Request an Editorial Board Meeting.* On a rare occasion, you may need to go to this length. If a major issue has received a lot of coverage and you feel that there have been serious errors or systematic unfair representation of your organization, you should consider requesting a meeting with the editorial board.

At this meeting, you can expect to see a high-ranking editor (if not the Editor-in-Chief), the bureau chief of your region, and any reporters who might cover your organization. Your delegation should include your highest-ranking officer, your media spokesperson, and one or two other individuals who have intimate knowledge of the particular issue at hand.

It is important that you do not go to such a meeting just to whine or to complain that someone at the paper does not like you or understand what a "good neighbor" you are trying to be. Instead, you should go to the meeting armed with your clippings book. On one occasion when I organized an Editorial Board meeting, I brought a 2" high pile of clippings from the past four months of coverage related to an inactive hazardous waste site on our property. I had used different color highlighter pens to indicate:

Pink—where the reporter had made a misstatement of fact or reported inaccurately

Green—where the reporter had strayed quite far into the area of opinion

Blue—where the story was actually fair and balanced but the headline writer had put a negative slant on things

Yellow—where the company's side of the story was either given short shrift or totally ignored

I calmly presented this information. With concrete

examples like this, the Editor-in-Chief had to agree that the treatment we had received was not in line with the highest principles of journalistic ethics. He listened when we provided background on the issue and detailed what the company was doing to correct the problem.

In our presence, this Editor-in-Chief also gave very explicit directions to the young reporters on our beat. They were told never again to assume it was too late at night and they should not bother me at home. (He was evidently impressed that I had given them my home phone number so we could always have an opportunity to comment on a story about us.)

As a result of this meeting, subsequent coverage on this subject and others was much more balanced, at least while those reporters and those editors were still at that location!

- *Take Out a Paid Advertisement.* If nothing else is working, or if you want to get immediate attention, you can pay for an ad. You've all seen these. When a company needs to apologize for a major *faux pas*, they often do this. If they want to draw attention to their position, they can do it in bold headlines. They can tell their story in their own words. To answer their critics, they can set up a Myth vs. Fact piece to set the record straight.

Sure it calls more attention to the controversy, but you have to weigh that against the advantage of being able to reach a wide audience with your message, stated your way.

As you have noticed, each of the listed options has advantages and disadvantages. Recognize what they are, consider them carefully, and then make your decision about the best course of action for your organization.

Athletes and astronauts understand the need to practice their skills regularly so that they can perform well when the pressure is on.

CHAPTER

27

Practice or Perish

I f you follow the advice provided up to this point, you will be better able to handle any crisis you may encounter, including the media attention that will accompany it.

However, there is something else you can do which will **maximize** the benefits of reading this book. Theories of adult learning state clearly that people absorb and retain MUCH more if they actively participate in the process as opposed to just hearing a lecture or reading a book.

The Value of Realistic Role-Plays

When I conduct my full-day workshops, the part that gets consistently high ratings is the role-playing exercise. All of the theory, tips and techniques of how to manage a crisis are delivered in the first part of the workshop. If participants were to walk out then, I dare say that months or even weeks later—if a crisis erupted—they would not be able to recall as much as they would like. True, they would have their handouts to refer to. Those of you who have read this book and kept it somewhere close by could reach for it to remind yourself of the basic principles.

But if you have an opportunity to PRACTICE what you learn

right after you learn it, I can guarantee that it will stick with you longer. In the role-playing portion of the workshop, I always present clients with scenarios that could **really** happen in their business. I spend a lot of time working with one of the managers ahead of time to see just what type of crises they worry about. (I used to hate it when practice exercises were given in seminars that didn't relate to me in the least. It made me feel stupid, then frustrated, and then angry.)

My clients tell me that when they see the role-plays I've developed for them, they immediately get caught up in the exercise. (Some say they actually begin to sweat!) They jump right in and start figuring out what they would need to do and say to the media or the assembled angry people. Sometimes they have given a lot of thought to certain possible crises they might actually face. My chemical industry friends usually think about accidental spills or a fire/explosion. Bank clients think of robberies or embezzlements. Hospitals and nursing homes are alert to situations where their staff could be accused of providing substandard care. Utilities are accustomed to dealing with issues of outages. Not-for-profits know they constantly need to be ready to assure donors that their funds are being used properly.

But I like to throw some unexpected role-plays at them. Anyone can be accused of sexual harassment/discrimination or unlawful firing; glitches can occur in the execution of an emergency response; violence in the workplace can occur in any organization; employees can engage in immoral or unlawful activities on their personal time which reflect negatively on the organization that hired them, etc. It is a good test of how well the participants can apply the crisis management principles they learned to these new situations.

Benefits of Practicing Scenarios

Working through these role-plays together has many other benefits:

(1) *Teamwork is enhanced.* Dealing with a crisis is not something that can be done in isolation. There is too much work to be done and too many audiences to communicate with for one individual to do it all. By playing out some of the situations in the role-plays, you will be able to see how people work together under stressful conditions. Managers will have an opportunity to see how their functional area interacts with and impacts others, especially when the pressure is on. Inevitably there is the Vice President of Operations who says, "Well, this is easy. All we would do in a case like this is ...." Then the Vice President of Marketing would say, "Wait a minute. You have to consider how our customers would react to that approach." Or the Human Resources Manager would say, "If we did what you suggest, we would surely have a lawsuit brought against us." How much better to work these things out in a role-play than in a real crisis!

I want to say a word here about how very important it is for the highest-ranking official of the organization to be present during this training and the role-plays. It is vital that this individual sees how his management team would respond to incidents of various kinds. He may have strong opinions and valuable insights based on his knowledge of the big picture. If the management team were to go off in a direction that made him uncomfortable, how much better for everyone to learn that while role-playing — before the real thing occurs! Many times CEO's are travelling and not immediately available in the first moments of a crisis. How much more efficient his subordinates would be if they were confident their approach to this type of crisis would have his blessing. What if they were only able to contact him just as they were ready to give their statement to the press and found out then that he disagreed totally? They would have to start all over again developing their response; many precious minutes of that critical first 1-2 hours would be lost. Or worse yet, what if the CEO only heard the organization's statement on the evening news, when there is little that can be done to repair the damage?

(2) *Staff abilities are showcased.* Several CEO's have told me that they learned a great deal about the skills and abilities of their management team by watching how they handled themselves in the scenarios we role-played. Whether it highlighted someone's particular strengths or pointed out an area of weakness that needed to be addressed, it was good that these things surfaced in a role-play.

(3) *Gaps in policies and procedures are uncovered.* So often the planning of a crisis response for a scenario will reveal utter confusion among the ranks. They discover that either no policies or procedures have been established, or that the policies are not clearly understood. The policy manual may have been sitting on a shelf for a long time. If no one has dusted it off and looked at it for years to see if the policies are still appropriate, or if the employees do not know what the policies are, they might as well not exist.

(4) *The management group gains confidence in their approach.* If the management team has had an opportunity to work through a particular kind of crisis during a role-play, just imagine how much more competently they will handle a crisis should it occur. I once had just such an experience. I trained the management team of a chemical company in March. One of the role-plays involved a fire in a warehouse near a residential area. Three weeks later, in mid-April, the plant manager called me.

"Judy, you will be so proud of us! Last night we had a fire in the warehouse just like we practiced last month. The newspaper article in today's paper was not only reasonable, but they spent the majority of the article talking about how competently the company handled both the incident and their communication with the media and the concerned neighbors. We cannot thank you enough for helping us look good!" Talk about the rewards of this business...

(5) *A lot less Monday-morning quarterbacking goes on.* If there are a reasonable number of people in the workshop (usually 9-12), each person gets an "opportunity" to fulfill the role of spokesperson. Everyone gets a chance to break out in a cold sweat, to feel the butterflies zooming around in their stomachs, and to experience a momentary brain-drain when the video camera light goes on. From the CEO, to the usual organization spokesperson, to the middle manager with special knowledge of the particular crisis being role-played, everyone on the "hot seat" will make a mistake. They will say something they wish they had not said. They will forget to verbalize one of their "must air" messages. They will betray, through nervous gestures, just how uncomfortable they are. No one will be perfect. As a result, they will not only be better prepared if they are ever called upon in a crisis situation, but they will also be a lot more sympathetic and supportive of the person who ends up with the job of spokesperson. They are just grateful that it wasn't them out there on the firing line!

Do You Absolutely Need to Pay a Consultant to Lead You Through This Process?

No. You can do it yourselves. One of the last things I do when finishing up a workshop is strongly recommend that the CEO make it a routine practice to put his management team through crisis scenarios on a regular basis. It could be part of a regular staff meeting. Or it could be the basis for calling a special meeting, just like a real crisis. Bring together your Crisis Management Team. Hand them a piece of paper that describes what has occurred. Give them 15-20 minutes to work out what actions they would take, whom they would notify, and what they would say to the press. Put a spokesperson up in the front of the room and simulate a media interview. Everyone agrees this is a great idea to help keep the learning fresh in their minds.

The problem is that I don't think many of my clients actually do it. Some of them know they should, but they just don't take the time. Of course I don't mind that many prefer to ask me to come back two years later and put them through the instruction and the scenarios again. (Often I find that there have been quite a few personnel changes, so this is valuable in more ways than one.)

The Advantages of Including a Media Training Expert

Sure you can do the role-playing on your own, even if you have never participated in such a workshop. You just should be aware that using a media training consultant has certain significant advantages:

(1) *They have a broader base of knowledge in this area.* You spend most of your working life dealing with other issues. This is not your area of expertise. You may not be aware of the pitfalls as well as someone who has seen similar situations in other companies. You may not realize how specific words you use in your statement might bring a negative reaction from the public. You wouldn't want a beginner to give you golf lessons or teach you to fly an airplane. Why would you settle for the advice of an amateur when your organization's reputation is on the line?

(2) *Media trainers do not have to be concerned about internal*

organizational politics. Another way to say this is that a consultant may be the only one who can speak up with impunity and tell the CEO that he's wrong. (The cartoon that draws the biggest laugh during my workshops is of the smug-looking CEO sitting at the head of the conference room table saying, "Now, all those opposed, signify by saying 'I quit!'") No matter how good the team is, or how open the management style, there still may be some hesitation about being totally honest with the boss. Somebody has to do this, especially when the organization is seeking to turn around a tense crisis situation.

(3) *Someone who has experience with a wide variety of organizations can more easily identify best practices.* A consultant who moves from company to company frequently can pick up ideas about how some of the more successful companies do things—ideas that can help your organization.

(4) *Things come up in the scenarios that may not have been covered in the actual training.* So much learning takes place in the role-playing of scenarios! No instructor can cover every possible point in the 3-4 hours of the instruction session. Numerous teaching opportunities present themselves in the course of the role-playing exercise. It is better to have a professional media trainer there to point them out and take the time to cover the issues.

Just as I was ready to submit this manuscript to the publisher, I was talking with my next-door neighbor about why organizations should want to contract with a consultant. She got the idea immediately. "It's like when you read a recipe from Martha Stewart in a magazine and decide to try it yourself," she said. "Most of the time, it doesn't work quite right. You're pretty sure Martha would not approve. Sometimes it is just plain awful. There is a big difference between reading something and trying to put it into practice on your own. You would much rather be able to watch the cook as she prepares the dish. Better yet, you could have her look over your shoulder as you try it on your own so she can correct you as you go and point out little nuances to techniques that you may not have thought about."

What a perfect analogy to make my point. Thanks, Tricia!

The Inestimable Value of Drills/Exercises

It is reasonable to expect people who do something every day to do it well. But we don't encounter a crisis every day. It may therefore not be reasonable for the public to expect that you can handle an unpredictable emergency well – BUT THEY DO!

Your only chance to succeed is if you exercise your plan and your response and do it frequently. Some people say that doing important things is "like riding a bike – you never forget." That simply is not true in the arena of preparing for a disaster or crisis. We rode a bike frequently when we were children and probably did it often as we grew older. How often do we practice responding in an emergency? Even Lance Armstrong couldn't take a year off between the Tour de France races and expect to be able to perform well.

Emergency responders are often sent to training classes. But if they don't have opportunities to put that training into practice in a real emergency or a realistic drill, they are not going to reap the most benefit.

The best way is to develop a planned, progressive exercise program. Several small drills could each focus on one part of the plan – alerting and activation, communications, testing of individual components, processes and equipment, etc. Then when the "bugs" have been worked out of the components, a full-scale drill should be scheduled that sees how everything works together.

Be sure, if you do the full-scale drill for an operational site, that you include coordination with corporate headquarters. Otherwise, you may find that – even though they want to help – corporate CMT members may make demands (usually for frequent communication) which actually hinder the site's ability to respond optimally. Much of this interface can be worked out to be less intrusive if it is thought about and practiced before it is really needed.

If you insist on burying your head in the sand,

just realize that a LOT of your anatomy is left exposed!

Keeping Cool on the Hot Seat

Few people enjoy being caught in the center of a crisis. When something bad has happened in our organizations, we don't like the sensation of losing control. When the media gets involved, this feeling is accentuated. For most of us, it is definitely not pleasant to be the one caught in the glare of the TV camera lights when tough questions are being asked. Many organizations would prefer not to plan for the times when they might need to deal with a crisis. Apparently, they believe that if they don't talk about it, nothing bad will happen to them.

Figure 11

I'm Glad That You are Not an Ostrich!

The fact that you are reading this book tells me that you do not belong in this category. You are aware that you need to be prepared. If you have followed my advice, you should feel confident that you will be able to move through the crisis with as little pain as possible.

- Section I helped you realize what you need to think about BEFORE a crisis hit.

- Section II provided you with ways to organize yourself so that you have a better chance of responding appropriately within the first 1-2 hours of the crisis. This will set the tone for the rest of your dealings with the media and, through them, to the public.

- Section III started you thinking about the various audiences you need to address and what their basic concerns are apt to be.

- Section IV prepared you with specific do's and don't for dealing with the media.

- Section V revealed the "tricks of the trade" that professional media trainers know about. Now you do too.

- Section VI made you aware of the importance of HOW you deliver your messages.

- Section VII emphasized the value of keeping your skills sharp by role-playing so you are ready to respond effectively at a moment's notice.

No One Crisis is Exactly Like Any Other

No one response fits all. Each crisis situation will have a different set of circumstances, different audiences, and different communication avenues that you can use to get your story out. You don't want to limit your communications to just the media. However, knowing how to effectively work with the media is a critical piece. Feeling more confident in your dealings with the media will provide you with a solid foundation for dealing with any crisis.

Nobody Said It Was Going to Be EASY!

When a crisis occurs in your organization, you will likely have big knots in your stomach. If it's a long, drawn out type of crisis, you may not sleep well for a while. There can even be a pervasive feeling of dread as you face each day, opening the newspaper first thing in the morning to see what horrible thing has been written about you and your organization.

But remember, **you are not alone.**

- It often happens that the staff of an organization is brought closer together when they face difficult times. They learn to draw on the strength of each other as they work as a team.

- You may find there are resources available within your industry or professional association that you never realized were there. It is often helpful to turn to them. It feels good to find out that the dues you've paid for all these years will finally pay off.

- There are professional crisis management consultants whose job it is to help you work through the issues. It is often good to get an objective assessment of the problem and advice on your proposed responses.

- If you are one who draws comfort from your religious faith, you may want to copy down on an index card (as I did) portions of Scripture or an inspirational quote. I used Psalm 91. "He will cover you with His feathers, and under His wings you will find refuge." Keeping that prominently displayed on my desk helped me keep my cool during some of the toughest crises I faced.

Your Goal: From "Danger" to "Opportunity"

Back in Chapter 2 we discussed how the Chinese characters for the word "crisis" stand for (1) danger and (2) opportunity. I hope that this has real meaning to you now.

Throughout the book you have seen examples of the danger if you don't handle a crisis properly. People in the middle of the bell curve described in Chapter 10 who were sympathetics, straddlers, or skeptics can lose respect for your organization if you don't do and say the right things and do it early in the crisis. If you REALLY mess up, you can even lose some of your supporters and turn more people into splenetics.

However, most people can forgive an organization which has an unfortunate incident—provided they respond well. If you move quickly to take the appropriate course of action and explain what you are doing in terms laypeople can understand, you may even have a rare opportunity to enhance your corporate reputation.

Nothing would make me happier than to know that what I've written will help you do this.

VIII

Lessons Learned: Dangers and Opportunities in Crisis

My colleague, Jim Lukaszewski, is fond of pointing out how CEO's and other high-ranking officers of organizations occasionally face "CDM's"—*Career Defining Moments*. In many cases, those CDM's occur when the individual is caught in the glare of the media spotlight for all the world to see.

Since my book was originally published in April of 2001, there have been many CDM's. Jeffrey Skilling, Kenneth Lay, Boston's Cardinal Law, and Martha Stewart undoubtedly wish they had done things a lot differently. Conversely, former New York City Mayor Rudy Giuliani gained national prominence and a reputation as an extremely effective leader by the way he handled himself and led the citizens of his city through shock and despair to hope and confidence. Hospitals caught in the Blackout of 2003 came out looking prepared to deal with the crisis.

I've included in this new section a number of magazine articles written in 2001-2003 on the lessons we can learn from these incidents.

There is no better test for a person's character than his or her behavior when something has been done wrong.

Crisis Response to Dumb Decisions

When dealing with corporate reputation management, good public relations professionals advise their employers or their clients that the executives and managers must FIRST be prepared to DO the right thing. THEN they find ways to communicate the facts. If a company is not willing to DO the right thing, no pile of well-crafted press releases or fancy wording in company brochures or annual reports about their mission statements or ethics is going to be able to make up for that.

Bad Things Happen

Unfortunately, organizations sometimes make dumb decisions. Whether because management is consciously trying to take shortcuts to increase profits, attempting to avoid embarrassment, or they simply didn't think far enough ahead about the consequences, actions are taken which they later regret. Some of them are relatively harmless. Others—like the intricate financial partnerships developed to hide huge losses at Enron or the decision of Arthur Andersen to shred documents to cover it up—are major. They have far-reaching consequences that severely impact the lives of thousands of innocent people.

When organizations make dumb decisions, a public crisis develops when media attention is focused on them. At that point, these organizations can respond in one of two ways. They can

• step up to the plate as quickly as possible, admit their mistake, apologize, promise to take steps to keep it from happening again, and find ways to make reparations to those who were victimized.

• OR, they can obfuscate, dance around, cover up, take the Fifth Amendment before Congress or say "No comment" to the press. By doing so, they dig themselves deeper and deeper into a hole until there is so much dirt around no one can clearly see the organization any more.

Accidents happen. People make mistakes in judgment. Equipment malfunctions. Procedures aren't followed precisely. Policies are allowed to get out of date or aren't followed closely. There are many reasons why bad things happen to organizations even when they are trying to do the right thing.

However, when there is no ethical center, when people in high positions are willing to shade the truth or outright lie, when the corporate culture is that the end justifies the means, then you have a prescription for disaster. A lot of innocent people can get hurt. The ramifications are far-reaching, even beyond the impacts on the employees or shareholders of that one organization. The negativity can carry over to a whole industry. Those who compose regulations to curtail such excesses can go too far and punish even more innocent people.

Examples of Bad and Good Handling of Crises

We are all aware of what happened to two huge companies who used to be well regarded. The reputations of both Enron and Arthur

Andersen went from stellar to the cellar. All of the facts about exactly who knew what when and what they did about it are still unknown as I write this, but it is obvious that a lot of dumb decisions were made by those who should have known better. We have seen the devastating results for those two companies and for the multitude of others those caught in the ripple effects—actually more like tidal waves. Employees lost jobs and watched their pension funds disappear. Investors, including elderly people who were dependent on this income, were left holding the bag. Congress passed regulations which are making life difficult for many honest accounting firms. There is plenty of misery to go around.

Contrast how the executives of these organizations handled their crises ("no comment" to the press, taking the Fifth Amendment before congressional hearings, Mr. Lay sending his wife onto a major TV network to try to plead his case of not knowing what was occurring in his company) with the way Lee Iacocca of Chrysler Corporation handled his crisis back in 1987 (pages 106-107). Mr. Iacocca's approach managed the crisis and brought the bad publicity to an end. In fact, the media was flabberghasted at his forthright approach, his admission of guilt, and his willingness to make amends in ways that were considered fair by the people involved. Had he tried to continue to defend indefensible practices, he would have only lengthened and deepened the crisis and further tarnished the corporation's brand name until people would not trust Chrysler again. As it was, the corporation's market share bounced back nicely and Mr. Iacocca was credited as a good leader and an honest man.

Too bad some of today's corporate leaders that we've been reading about in the newspapers so frequently didn't learn a lesson from his example.

"People will forgive a screw-up but they won't forgive a cover-up."

Steve Hayworth
V.P. of Public Relations, CNN

30

What the Catholic Church Did Wrong

When the sexual abuse scandal in the Catholic church broke wide open, I was often asked my opinion of how the hierarchy was handling the situation. Although it distresses me to add to the pain being experienced by the many good Catholics (both the majority of priests and the many members of that faith), I feel that there are some important lessons we can draw from this tragedy.

Here, in my opinion, are some of the mistakes made by the hierarchy of the Catholic Church.

1. They did not face up to the problem immediately when it first appeared.

Allegations of sexual misconduct perpetrated on young boys by some priests were made years ago. There were opportunities then for the church to admit that inappropriate actions had occurred. When evidence of illegal or immoral or unethical behavior becomes known, organizations have a window of opportunity to step up and do the right thing, painful as it may be at that time. If these early allegations had been made public and the perpetrators prosecuted, things would surely have been much different. The Church should have stepped forward early to apologize for these actions, taken the criticism and a few negative news stories, compensated the victims, and gone on record (both within the church body and publicly) to emphasize that this type of conduct would not be tolerated.

This was not done. Because they were trying to avoid embarrassing news stories, decisions were evidently made to pay victims for their pledge of silence. The offending priests were not dealt with according to the law of the land. They were simply transferred to another unsuspecting community.

The more often it happened, the more embarrassing it was for the church to admit. The situation compounded itself and grew and grew until it inevitably burst open. Instead of an isolated case of wrongdoing that could be forgiven, it had become a system of deception that the public found inexcusable. As Steve Hayworth, V.P. of Public Relations for CNN said, "People will forgive a screw-up but they won't forgive a cover-up." The breadth and depth of this cover-up was huge and the public was enraged.

2. Lack of appearance of compassion for the victims.

One of the most important things that organizations must do in the earliest stages of any crisis is to indicate their care and concern for those who have been hurt, whether the damage has been physical, emotional, economic or psychological. They must not only BE sorry; they must SAY they are sorry. Often the victims desperately need an admission of guilt and a heartfelt apology. In some cases, the victims might have forgone a lawsuit if the guilty party admitted he was genuinely sorry.

What often happens, however, is that organizations are persuaded that an apology will lead to lawsuits, so they avoid saying that they deeply regret what has happened to innocent people. In a situation such as that faced by the Catholic Church, lawsuits were inevitable. When members of the church hierarchy used their time in the media spotlight not to apologize and express concern, but to defend their actions and raised the specter of bankruptcy, they threw away the opportunity to express their horror and dismay that priests had betrayed the trust of their parishioners.

3. Refusal to take responsibility and to commit to make things better.

Human nature demands that someone accept responsibility when something goes wrong. The media and the public always want to know "Who is to blame?" In this instance, both the offending priests and their superiors were at fault. The church leaders failed to take definitive action to limit the damage to young men and their families. People want to see an appropriate level of contrition. Beyond that, they want to see accompanying actions to preclude similar situations from occurring again. They will not accept any organization that tries to maintain that they are, in any way, above the law. Those who attempt to make that case will be perceived as arrogant and elitist, not something that goes down well with anyone. The public will continue to demand fair treatment of those injured (legal settlements) and punishment for those who should have taken action when the transgressions first became known (removal of certain people from office).

In this sad chapter in American history, you can't find any bright spots. The best thing you can do is learn from another organization's mistakes in order to avoid them yourself.

Never fear criticism when you are right;
never ignore it when you are wrong.

—Anonymous

31

What Can We Learn from Martha Stewart?

M en, keep reading! You may not want to learn how to turn leaves from your front lawn into a decorative centerpiece or how to effortlessly prepare a gourmet dinner for 24 with what's found in your pantry. However, you definitely can learn what NOT to do when it comes to handling a crisis! Martha may be a master of many things, but she obviously had no clue what to do when the investigative reporters and the Securities and Exchange Commission (SEC) came knocking. In fact, she made several classic mistakes – mistakes which ended up hurting her personal and corporate reputation as well as her financial assets.

1. She did not do the right thing. In many situations in life, there are right ways and wrong ways to do things. Whether you are a business executive/manager in a large corporation, a priest, an administrator in a health care facility, or a small businessperson, there are certain ethical and moral imperatives. Many of these things we should have learned at our mother's knee: don't cheat, follow the Golden Rule, tell the truth, etc. If you operate a publicly-owned company, there are strict regulations governing what you can and cannot do. Martha is a savvy businesswoman. She must have known that acting on the "tip" she received from her friend, the head of ImClone Systems, was a violation of SEC regulations. (NOTE: It has been estimated that, had she held on to the stock until the public announcement, she would have lost about $45,000—insignificant considering her net worth.) If one acts unethically, one has to take the consequences. No amount of crisis management technique or public relations "spin" is going to be able to compensate for the fact that a person DOES the wrong thing. As former President Lyndon B. Johnson once said, "You can't make chicken salad out of chicken _____ (manure)."

2. She did not admit her error immediately. Even if you make a bad decision and act improperly, there is a window of opportunity where you can admit your mistake and accept the consequences. The longer you deny wrongdoing, the deeper you get into lies and cover-ups. Delay causes more damage to your credibility and more negative publicity. Washington Post columnist Richard Cohen theorized that Martha, who had a reputation of being able to do everything perfectly (much to the dismay of most women I know), was not able to bring herself to admit publicly that she had done something wrong.

Ego is not limited to celebrities like Martha Stewart. Many CEO's and senior managers feel that they must always be right. Admitting a mistake is not easy. But look at the disastrous results in Martha's case! As of the date of this writing, it is not yet known exactly what her punishment will be in terms of penalties and possibly jail time. What IS known is that her reputation as an honest businesswoman has been dealt a terrible blow. Advertisers have dropped her product lines. Her name has been taken off the marquee of her own company. Cohen estimates that the financial damage which initially would have cost her $45,000 amounted to something like $360 million by mid-2003.

3. She did not ask for forgiveness. Some people find it very difficult to ask for forgiveness. These folks fail to realize that most people are ready to forgive a human failing if honestly admitted. When people quickly admit their mistakes and ask for forgiveness from those they have wronged, the ugly news story ends sooner. It can often be limited to one news cycle instead of being dragged out for days, weeks or even months. Perpetrators who continue to deny their mistakes appear arrogant, and the public and the judicial system want to see them taken down a peg or two.

In my workshops on handling the media during a crisis, I use the example of the Captain of the USS Greenville whose submarine surfaced incorrectly and tragically caused the death of nine Japanese fishermen. Against the advice of his lawyers, he personally went to the families of the dead fishermen, admitted his error and humbly begged their forgiveness. The reaction of most family members was that, once they witnessed his sincere contrition and genuine tears, they saw him as another human being, not a faceless cold monolith, and their anger dissipated. When someone has to be dragged, kicking and screaming, to talk with those wronged, it is a whole different story; the breach may never be healed.

In summary, the best course of action is to DO the right thing. Act ethically and legally so you won't get caught up in situations that bring you negative public and media attention. But if you mess up for some reason, have a lapse in judgment, or are tempted beyond your ability to withstand in a moment of weakness, have the decency and good sense to admit it as quickly as possible. Ask for forgiveness and move to make restitution if possible. In this way you will be able to put the misery behind you and go forward to start rebuilding your credibility. Don't let Martha Stewart be your role model.

"Some of the facts are true, some are distorted,

and some are untrue."

–A State Department Spokesman,
commenting on an article in "Foreign Policy"

CHAPTER
32

What Rudy Giuliani Did Right After the World Trade Center Attacks

After reading so much in this section on what organizations have done wrong when faced with a crisis, let's end on a positive note and look at someone who did things right, even in the face of one of the most horrible crises imaginable.

Prior to September 11, 2001, when was the last time you heard of a politician having an 85-90% approval rating? Probably never. Former NYC Mayor Rudy Giuliani achieved this because of his strong yet compassionate leadership in the aftermath of the terrorist attacks on his city.

Through my tears for the human tragedy that was unfolding just 50 miles from my home and devastating many families from my area, I also watched from the more detached perspective of a crisis management consultant. I was interested to see how the Mayor would communicate during this period of monumental crisis. I'd like to share some thoughts on what I observed. Perhaps it will help you prepare yourself for less catastrophic but still distressing crises that could occur in your organization.

In Chapter 13, I covered "The 10 C's of Good Crisis Communications." Here we will look at each one of them and see how Mayor Giuliani demonstrated his grasp of each.

1. Be COOPERATIVE: The Mayor knew from years of experience that he had to make himself personally available to the press immediately. Any attempt to avoid or delay meeting with reporters who were under the gun to relate the latest news would have led to miscommunication, rumor, and possibly panic.

2. Maintain CONTROL: He and his staff quickly set up a room for the media where they could be assured he would come to report the latest news. You do not want the media wandering around, getting in the way of emergency responders or officials trying to do their jobs.

3. Demonstrate CARING AND CONCERN: Expressions of compassion for those who have been victimized by an incident are always in order. Don't let your lawyers talk you out of this because they are afraid it will be interpreted as an admission of legal liability. (This was not as big of a concern for the Mayor when the whole city was a victim of an outside terrorist group as it would be if your organization could be perceived as being even partially to blame for the crisis.) Work with your legal advisors to find the best ways to word your expressions of condolence and comfort, but be sure to show kindness. Judges tend to throw the book at organizations which appear callous and uncaring. In almost every message in the early weeks of the crisis, the Mayor continued to express and demonstrate his deep sympathy for those affected and his desire to do what he could to help.

4. Display COMPETENCE: Some executives and managers believe that, because they have achieved a position of authority, they somehow will know instinctively what to do and say in a crisis. Many have learned that, sadly, this is not the case. Planning, preparation, and practice promote competence. When David Letterman asked the Mayor on his show one evening two weeks later how he seemed to always know the right things to do and say, Rudy's answer was, "We DRILL on these things." He did not mean by that remark that anyone in his administration had ever posed a scenario even remotely as far-reaching as this one. But they DID have a plan and his staff understood and accepted the ways they had been trained to respond to emergencies of various sorts. Because they had often had emergency drills, they at least had a solid framework on which they could build. As the citizens saw the Mayor and his team moving purposefully to do what was needed, they were admired as good leaders, competent to help them through this crisis.

5. Be CREDIBLE: There are two major components of credibility. The first is to never lie. Hiding or even shading the truth will come back to haunt you. Some days after September 11th, even when the families of the victims did not want to hear the truth, the Mayor had to tell them the chances of rescuing anyone alive were extremely remote. The other aspect of credibility has to do with not speculating. Even though the media pushed for definite answers to important questions, if the Mayor did not have certain knowledge, he refused to be stampeded into an answer just to satisfy them.

6. Be CONSISTENT: Speak with one voice. Be on the same page. Get your story straight. These are some phrases used to express this vital component of crisis communications. If a situation is long-term, where several spokespersons must be used, they must all coordinate their messages to prevent confusion; otherwise people will believe that things are not quite as represented. Even slightly different versions can damage credibility. The Mayor and his deputies/department heads obviously briefed each other every time prior to appearing in front of the media.

7. Speak with CLARITY: Several things come into play here. Even when exhaustion is inevitable due to lack of sleep, try not to mumble. Do not use jargon or technical language. If a 5 cent word expresses your thought well, do not use a 50 cent word because you think it will impress people. Your goal is to communicate clearly. The Mayor talked to the people in words they could understand – not beneath them like they were children, but not above their ability to comprehend.

8. Be CONCISE: This is a skill that comes with practice. The public does not want long drawn-out detailed explanations in the first throes of a crisis. They want the basic facts. The media is looking for "sound bites" – concise, memorable descriptions that conjure up a mental picture and lead to understanding. If your major message is buried among unimportant details, it may all end up on the editor's cutting room floor. Rudy was excellent in his ability to respond with answers that were to the point and quotable. For example, reporters naturally asked, among their first questions, if the Mayor had any idea how many people might have been killed. He did not waste time explaining how impossible that would be to know. He silenced them by telling them the number would be "more than we can bear."

9. Keep CURRENT: Reporters have to know for a fact that, if they stay in the designated media center, they will be kept up to date with the latest developments. If too much time passes between briefings, they will become impatient and wander off to talk to other sources – anyone who will grant an interview. The Mayor held frequent briefings to provide updates. He knew that literally the world was waiting to hear the latest information.

10. Act with CALM: Note this does not say "BE calm." In a serious crisis, it would be a rare individual who would not be anxious.

In the case of Rudy Giuliani, who came very close to being trapped in a building himself when the Twin Towers began to crumble, it is a testimony to his ability to lead in crisis that he was able to appear calm in the face of what he had just seen happening all around him. But a person who can demonstrate a steady confidence is highly regarded. Mayor Giuliani credits what he calls the concept of "relentless preparation" for his ability to act calmly. As he said in his book, *Leadership*: "Leaders may possess brilliance, extraordinary vision, fate, even luck. Those help; but no one, no matter how gifted, can perform without careful preparation…"

If your organization experiences a crisis of any kind, you would be well served to remember the example set by Mayor Giuliani as he led New York City through some of the darkest days any of us could ever imagine.

Some people change their ways when they see the light;
others wait until they feel the heat.

–Anonymous

33

The Blackout of '03

I n the electrical blackout of August 14-15, 2003 that plagued
millions of people, hospitals generally came out looking good.
Why? Because they were prepared for this specific possibility and
therefore were better able to cope with the situation. What can
other organizations learn from their example?

Hospitals Were Prepared for Loss of Power

As I listened to the radio on the afternoon of August 14th, one
of the very first things reporters were talking about was whether hospitals were affected. Were critical services interrupted causing heart-
rending tragedies? Would the hospitals be able to respond if there
were a rash of traffic accidents or a heavy influx of injuries in sub-
ways and elevators? How about broken arms or legs suffered when
people fell down dark stairwells? Word came very quickly that hospitals were functioning well. This was reassuring to the general public.

This did not happen by accident. It was a classic case of good
crisis planning. Many years ago, people who work in hospitals identified loss of electrical power as a major vulnerability with drastic
consequences. It was rather obvious that, if hospitals lost power,

critical pieces of equipment would stop running and lives could be lost within minutes. Agreement was easy to come by—this could not be allowed to happen. Therefore steps were taken to provide hospitals with back-up generators which could carry the electrical load required to run critical lights and equipment.

What About Other Vulnerabilities?

I would like to recommend that all types of organizations look at this example, but take it even further to identify and plan for other types of crises. The first thing you need is a "vulnerability audit."

In such an audit, you are trying to ferret out the things that would have the greatest negative impact on the organization and the population it serves. You do this by surveying a number of people in the organization. The survey can be written or verbal (as long as only a small group of people are asking the questions to maintain consistency). Ask about any potential problems the organization is currently facing or may likely face in the future. You should probe a bit, asking questions related to the physical plant, the staffing, procedures, regulatory requirements, public perceptions, and plans for the future. Be sure to ask a wide cross-section of people, not just senior managers. You can even extend it outside the organization to customers, Board members, major suppliers. This avoids "group think," which may tend to sweep problems under the rug.

Ranking the Vulnerabilities

Consolidate the answers that seem to be closely related. Next, rank them. An effective way to do this is to lay out a grid where the vulnerabilities are placed somewhere on the chart shown on the next page. First rate on the one axis the severity (either in terms of a devastating impact on a small number of individuals or the fact that a large number of people would be put at risk). Then rate on the other axis the likelihood that such an event might occur.

You can ask a smaller group of people to participate in this ranking exercise. However, it should not be left to just one person. Too many critical judgments must be made. Ask each person to assign a value from 1-10 on each axis and plot the point where they intersect.

For example, in the hospital setting cited at the beginning, a major power outage which would cause lights to shut off in operating rooms and cause life-sustaining pieces of equipment to fail would rank at the top right hand corner with a 10-10 rating. Having a doctor or nurse unknowingly spreading a contagious disease might get a rating of 8-3 (serious impact on some people but a low probability of happening).

What to Do Next?

Once the vulnerabilities are laid out on the grid, you should immediately address the things that show up in the upper right hand quadrant. Spend some time deciding what you could do to prevent this from happening. Is there equipment that needs to be bought and installed (like the back-up generators)? Do policies need to be drawn up and disseminated? Do people need to be trained on what to do if this should occur despite their best efforts? Does everyone know what their role would be if this crisis occurred and who should be called upon for help (and how to get in touch with them)?

When you've addressed the highest ranked vulnerability, move on to the next most dangerous one. Keep doing this until you have addressed AT LEAST three of the four quadrants, leaving out the one that has low severity and low probability.

The public (and the media) expect you to be ready to handle any crisis. Following this recommendation will provide you with the assurance that you have applied a systematic approach to assessing your potential risk and give you a better chance of being able to respond quickly and efficiently because you will be prepared.

A Case in Point

The Lord works in mysterious ways. As I was in the home stretch of preparing this manuscript, I had a stressful and upsetting experience. When I looked back on it, however, I realized that there were many important lessons to be learned about how to prepare for and handle a crisis—even though the media did not get involved. Let me explain.

When Everything Has to Work Right, Something Doesn't

It was one of those winter days in New York State that makes you wish you hadn't scheduled a business meeting. Several inches of snow had fallen overnight, so it was a real effort for my husband to get our rather large driveway shoveled so I could get out. We decided it would be safer for me to take his SUV.

Just as I turned into the entrance of the business park where I was headed, I began to hear a funny noise. By the time I got to a parking place, I realized that my right front tire was completely flat. Here was a mini-crisis. Eight men from a government-sponsored technology development center were going to be gathering in a conference room within ten minutes. I was expected to give them a presentation on what services my consulting business could offer to the businesses with which they came into contact each day. I very much wanted to make a good impression so they would remember me as a professional whom they could confidently recommend to their clients.

Okay, I said to myself. I'm a crisis management consultant. Surely I should be able to handle this. Let me tell you how things went.

The Best Laid Plans...

First and foremost, it was reassuring to remember that my husband and I had done some pre-crisis planning. We figured out twenty years ago that we should be prepared for the day when something would go wrong with one of our vehicles while we were traveling. So we joined an automobile club that provided roadside assistance with just one phone call. In the past twenty years, we had called upon it only two other times: once for another flat tire and once when a set of keys got locked inside the car. The annual fees for our coverage have added up to a considerable sum over these twenty years. But we always had the peace of mind that comes from knowing help was just a phone call away. That was a good thing.

I knew that the membership card with the phone number was in my wallet, right where I had placed it in case of such an emergency. I figured I'd just go in the office and make one phone call and be well on my way to solving the crisis.

But, wait! Where *was* that membership card with the telephone number? It *should* have been in my wallet. It's been there for years. A frenzied search through other parts of the wallet and my credit card case came up empty. Then I remembered. In preparation for a business trip several weeks previously, in an effort to lighten the load in my always-too-heavy purse, I went through and took out a bunch of things I wouldn't need on the trip. That membership card was one of them. I hadn't put it back when I came home.

I knew whom I was supposed to call, but I didn't have ready access to their telephone number, so I couldn't implement my plan. (Remember my advice to always have available the telephone numbers of those you will need to contact?)

Of course, there was another way I could get the number. I had been planning not to even bother my husband with this problem since there was little he could do about it from far away. But now I had to contact him and ask him to look on his card. My heart sank when he was not at home. Fortunately, I knew where he might be and had memorized his mother's phone number. I was able to reach him there. He gave me the telephone number.

All set, right? Two minutes to go until my presentation was to begin. I could make it. I was relieved when the road service people picked up on the second ring. What was their first question? "What is your member number so we can verify your coverage?" Of course I didn't know it. I only used it two times in twenty years! Why hadn't I thought to ask my husband that question that, in hindsight, was so obvious? Because, in the heat of the crisis, I wasn't thinking as clearly as I should have. That's not unusual. But it makes you feel dumb, and gets you more flustered.

After another phone call to my husband, and with the member number available, I started to dial the road service people again. Out of the corner of my eye, I could see folks starting to head for the conference room, expecting to see me there. Just one phone call to go. What's that beeping noise? My cell phone battery was going dead!

Then I remembered something else. Some months previously, I had sensed that the cell phone battery was not holding its charge nearly as long as it used to. In fact, I had called the manufacturer and ascertained that batteries usually last anywhere from 12-18 months on my model. Mine was 18 months old. Wanting to be prepared, I ordered a new one. Where was it now when I really needed it? Safely tucked away in my office desk drawer waiting for the old one to really die. Being frugal with my business funds, you could call it. Or you could call it foolish. What if I were to need my cell phone in an emergency some day? Oh, that won't happen. I'll have plenty of warning. Yeah, right… It made me think of the various crises in industry that have been caused when a company tries to stretch the periods between doing some preventative maintenance or puts off buying a new piece of equipment, hoping that the old one will give them just "one more year until we're in a better financial position."

This problem, too, could be solved with an alternative approach. There were phones in the office where I was visiting and they didn't mind if I used one to call the 800 number. Then the roadside assistance operator asked me, "Where can we reach you to let you know the tow truck is outside ready to help you?" I couldn't give them my cell phone number because it was dead. The charger for my host's cell phone wouldn't fit mine. With all of us in the conference room, no one would hear the phone ring at the central receptionist's desk. She was out sick with the flu.

My host said he would be glad to let me provide his cell phone number to the road service representative, but his phone was out in his car. By now, of course, it was raining. Make that pouring. He was nice enough to go out and get his phone for me, but my level of embarrassment was rising astronomically.

I gave the number to the operator. She said, "Someone should be there within 45 minutes to an hour." Great, I thought. That timing should be just about right. These guys won't want to hear me for more than 45 minutes anyway.

So I went in, just five minutes late, and started making my presentation by apologizing for keeping them waiting. Just a half-hour into the presentation, when they were asking me some great questions, the cell phone rang. "The tow truck operator is in the parking lot. Can you go right down?" I kicked myself for not telling them to be sure not to come for at least an hour. Hindsight. It always shows you things you should have done but didn't think of in the heat of the moment when a hundred other things were clamoring for your attention.

Too late now. I stayed for a few more minutes and tried to tie things up as best I could. Of course I was distracted and I'm not sure what kind of impression I made. I had to go. The tow truck operator wouldn't wait forever. I couldn't afford for him to get disgusted and leave because I had to get back to my office for some other commitments later in the day.

Actually Solving the "Crisis" Wasn't All That Hard

Luckily, when I got to the car, he was still there and not too upset about my keeping him waiting. A flat tire didn't fluster him. He'd been through this drill literally hundreds of times before. He had knowledge of the procedures required to solve the problem and was strong enough to carry them out. He also had enough experience with similar problems to be able to figure out how to use the special tools required to release the spare tire from underneath this type of vehicle. (At least I had the Owner's Manual readily available in the glove compartment, just in case.)

As is often the case with other types of crises, the actual mitigation of the problem is not so hard if you have skilled and dedicated people, clear procedures and the right equipment. It is usually the communications issues that foul things up.

Communications Issues Common to All Crises

That is why I have written this book. I wouldn't know how to solve the specific types of crises that may occur in your day-to-day operations. Even though I worked in the chemical industry for seventeen years, I could not begin to tell anyone how to safely clean up a hazardous material spill. My knowledge of banking consists of how to make deposits and (more frequently) withdrawals, and balance my checkbook. My only experience with hospitals has been as a visitor except for two instances of delivering babies. Everything I know about administering a nursing home comes only from the perspective of being with my father every day for the last two weeks of his life. My experience with electricity is limited to turning switches on and off and changing light bulbs. If it's anything more complicated than that, I'm pretty well lost. I believe in supporting not-for-profit agencies as much as I can, but I have little idea of how they operate.

However, the communications issues for crises in all of these types of organizations are very much the same. Basic principles apply. I've witnessed this for a fact. Normally I provide my workshop for the management team of one facility or for 2-3 people from several sites drawn together from one corporation. On several occasions, however, I have been asked to conduct a workshop under the auspices of a Chamber of Commerce or a local manufacturing council. In attendance at the same session have been people from chemical companies, various manufacturers, not-for-profit agencies, hospitals, banks, nursing homes, retailers, and propane distributorships. Each brings his own frame of reference to the class. Each learns the principles of good communication and can apply the techniques to his particular type of organization and gain insights from seeing how others deal with their issues.

How Prepared Are You for Your Next Crisis?

I hope the sharing of my flat tire experience will encourage you to think about the preparations you have made in your organization. When something unexpected happens, will you have the communications systems in place to cope with it? In the grand scheme of things, there was not much at risk in my situation. My whole business did not depend on making a good impression at this one meeting. Nobody was injured. The environment was not threatened.

In your business, the stakes are higher. People or the environment could be damaged. Lives could be unalterably affected. A lot of money could be wasted. People could lose their jobs if your organization were not to survive the crisis. A great deal is riding on your ability to (1) prevent a crisis from occurring and (2) if it does happen, mitigate the crisis as quickly as possible and communicate effectively with all of the appropriate audiences in order to minimize the damage.

You will not be able to do this effectively if you have to start learning all about how to handle a crisis after it has already hit. One of my colleagues told me about his past experience as an ice hockey referee. "We would mock any referee who came to the game with the rule book in his back pocket. If you don't know all the rules before you get into the game, you shouldn't be on the ice!"

I hope I've been able to help you succeed in your efforts to be well prepared and to have more confidence that you could deal effectively with the media in a crisis. I also hope that you will contact me should you feel that you would like further training. If you have any success (or horror!) stories which you would be willing to share, I hope you will let me know.

A thought I remembered when deep in a crisis that brought

me comfort and hope: "But they that wait upon the Lord

shall renew their strength. They shall mount up with wings

like eagles; they shall run and not be weary; they shall walk

and not faint."

Isaiah 40:31

APPENDIX
A Generic Statement

(Your City, the Date): This is the information we can confirm at this time. At _____, we experienced

_____

(Provide as many facts as can be confirmed: who, what, where, when, how.) As a result, ___ employees were injured and have been transported to _____ where they are undergoing treatment. Company officials have notified the families and are at the hospital to offer their support.

We are grateful to our employees and the local emergency agencies who responded so quickly and effectively to successfully control the situation. At no time was there a danger posed to the surrounding community.

At this moment, it is too early to determine the specific cause of the accident. Company personnel are cooperating completely with local authorities. The safety of our employees and our neighbors is extremely important to _____. We are committed to conducting a thorough investigation of the incident to learn what can be done to minimize the chance of anything like this happening again. When the cause is established, we will be in touch with the appropriate authorities to discuss our findings.

For further information, contact _____.

INDEX

SUGGESTED READINGS

Beat the Press by Shirley Fulton and Al Guyant
Published by American Book Business Press, 2002
Available at www.BeatThePress.net

Both authors worked as journalists and public information offi-cers for various institutions. In Chapters 9-17, they provide dozens of examples of clearly thought-out and well-worded answers to tough questions that you could be asked in various sticky situations.

MediaSmart: How to Handle a Reporter (By a Reporter)
by Dennis Stauffer
Published by MinneApplePress, 1994
Available at *www.amazon.com*

Dennis held numerous positions in TV news over 14 years. The book is full of valuable insights of how to work with reporters for your mutual benefit. He teaches you, through interesting anec-dotes, how to recognize and avoid the pitfalls you could encounter. By following his advice you can, as he says, "be caught in the headlines without being caught in the headlights."

James E. Lukaszewski is one of the most highly respected crisis management experts in the country. He is also a prolific writer. Over two dozen of his books and monographs which provide invaluable advice on avoiding and dealing with a crisis can be accessed by going to *www.amazon.com* and entering his name. You can also browse through Jim's extensive web site at *www.e911.com*

If you ever encounter upset, angry or hostile people -- either in your professional or personal life -- this CD Workshop is for you!

- Angry customers mean lost business.
- Upset colleagues lead to negative morale.
- Strong disagreements in families make for a stressful home life.

Learning this simple four-step process of "Taking the HEAT" will allow you to diffuse the anger and restore peace and harmony to important relationships.

Judy Hoffman is a consultant who specializes in dealing with the media and with upset people, especially during crisis situations. She provides workshops and speeches on these topics at conferences and association meetings nationwide and is a frequent contributor to numerous publications around the country. Her clients include many in the chemical industry as well as managers and executives of hospitals, banks, utilities, telecommunications companies, manufacturers, and not-for-profit agencies. You can find out more about her at her web site at www.JudyHoffman.com or by calling 1-800-848-3907 PIN 2145.

Mike Landrum is an accomplished actor and speech coach who helps individuals improve both their writing and speaking skills. You can contact him at www.CoachMike.com.

"Judy's presentation was a great conference opener, very relevant to the audience."

Jennifer Poinsett, Manager of Meetings Petroleum Marketers Assoc. of America

"Without exception, everyone who attended found your information easy to understand and extremely useful. You have empowered us with the knowledge and skills to deal with upset clients."

Ellyn Cohen, Director of Public Relations and Marketing JCC-Y of Rockland County, NY

Order online at www.JudyHoffman.com, or complete the form below:

Your Company Name:_____

Your name: _____

Mailing address:_____

City: _____ State:_____ Zip:_____

Phone: _____ E-Mail:_____

Type of payment: __ Visa __ Mastercard __ American Express

Credit Card #:_____ Exp. date:_____

Signature:_____

Pricing:
(1-3) at $12.95 - (4-11) at $9.95

No. of copies: _____ x $ _____ = _____
Shipping & Handling ($2 per book)
(NYS Residents add tax)

TOTAL DUE:

Fax this form to:
845.928.3463

Mail this form with payment to:
JCH Enterprises
25 Jones Drive
Highland Mills, NY 10930

You can also order on-line at:
www.JudyHoffman.com

Book Order Form

If you would like to order more copies of this book, please use the order form below. Discounts are available for carton-lot orders.

Orders should be sent (and checks made payable) to:
JCH Enterprises
25 Jones Drive
Highland Mills, NY 10930
Phone: 845-928-8239
Fax: 845-928-3463
e-mail: jchent@fcc.net

Please send me _____ copies of *Keeping Cool on the Hot Seat* at $21.95 each.

_____ copies x $21.95 (incl. S&H) ————

Add $2.00 per copy for Priority Mail ————

Residents of New York, add appropriate sales tax ————

TOTAL: ————

Name (Please print) _____

Company _____

Street Address or PO Box _____

City _____ State _____ Zip _____

Call for information regarding carton lot discounts

___ **Check here if you would like information on media training and crisis management workshops**

___ **Note: Consideration is being given to recording this book on audio tape. If you might be interested, please check here, fill out this information and send it via fax to (845) 928-3463**